C0-CZY-913

CURRENT ISSUES IN
LINGUISTIC THEORY

JANUA LINGUARUM

STUDIA MEMORIAE
NICOLAI VAN WIJK DEDICATA

edenda curat

CORNELIS H. VAN SCHOONEVELD

STANFORD UNIVERSITY

SERIES MINOR
38

1970

MOUTON
THE HAGUE · PARIS

CURRENT ISSUES IN LINGUISTIC THEORY

410.18
C 454

c. 2

by

NOAM CHOMSKY
M.I.T.

Fifth Printing

105027

1970

MOUTON
THE HAGUE · PARIS

LIBRARY ST. MARY'S COLLEGE

© *Copyright 1964 in The Netherlands.*
Mouton & Co. N.V., Publishers, The Hague

No part of this book may be translated or reproduced in any form,
by print, photoprint, microfilm, or any other means, without written
permission from the publishers.

First Printing 1964
Second Printing 1966
Third Printing 1967
· Fourth Printing 1969

A revised and expanded version of a report presented to the session: "The logical basis of linguistic theory", Ninth International Congress of Linguists, Cambridge, Mass., 1962.

repl. of # 82770

Printed in The Netherlands by Mouton & Co., Printers, The Hague.

TABLE OF CONTENTS

1. GOALS OF LINGUISTIC THEORY   7

2. LEVELS OF SUCCESS FOR GRAMMATICAL DESCRIPTION . . .   28
   2.0 28
   2.1 Levels of Adequacy in Phonology 30
   2.2 Levels of Adequacy in Syntax   34
   2.3 Levels of Adequacy in Semantics   50
   2.4 Comprehensiveness of Grammars   52

3. ON OBJECTIVITY OF LINGUISTIC DATA   56

4. THE NATURE OF STRUCTURAL DESCRIPTIONS   60
   4.0 60
   4.1 The Syntactic Component   60
   4.2 The Phonological Component   65
   4.3 Taxonomic Phonemics   75
   4.4 Criteria for Systematic Phonemics   95
   4.5 The Motivation for Taxonomic Phonemics   97

5. MODELS OF PERCEPTION AND ACQUISITION   111

BIBLIOGRAPHY   114

1

GOALS OF LINGUISTIC THEORY

1.0. In this paper,[1] I will restrict the term "linguistic theory" to systems of hypotheses concerning the general features of human language put forth in an attempt to account for a certain range of linguistic phenomena. I will not be concerned with systems of terminology or methods of investigation (analytic procedures). ⌐The central fact to which any significant linguistic theory must address itself is this: a mature speaker can produce a new sentence of his language on the appropriate occasion, and other speakers can understand it immediately, though it is equally new to them.⌐ Most of our linguistic experience, both as speakers and hearers, is with new sentences; once we have mastered a language, the class of sentences with which we can operate fluently and without difficulty or hesitation is so vast that for all practical purposes (and, obviously, for all theoretical purposes), we may regard it as infinite. Normal mastery of a language involves not only the ability to understand immediately an indefinite number of entirely new sentences, but also the ability to identify deviant sentences and, on occasion, to impose an interpretation on them.[2] It is evident that

[1] This work was supported in part by the U.S. Army Signal Corps, the Air Force Office of Scientific Research, and the Office of Naval Research, and in part by the National Science Foundation (Grant G-13903).
The account of linguistic structure sketched below in part incorporates, and in part developed in response to many stimulating ideas of Zellig Harris and Roman Jakobson. Its present form is to a large extent a product of collaboration over many years with Morris Halle, to whom (along with Paul Postal and John Viertel) I am indebted for much helpful criticism of this paper. For references, see the bibliography at the end of the paper.
[2] Cf. Chomsky (1955, chapter 4; 1961b), Ziff (1961), Putnam (1961), Miller and Chomsky (1963). Apparently many linguists hold that if a context can be constructed in which an interpretation can be imposed on an utterance, then it follows that this utterance is not to be distinguished, for the purposes of study of grammar, from perfectly normal sentences. Thus, e.g., "colorless green ideas

rote recall is a factor of minute importance in ordinary use of language, that "a minimum of the sentences which we utter is learnt by heart as such – that most of them, on the contrary, are composed on the spur of the moment," and that "one of the fundamental errors of the old science of language was to deal with all human utterances, as long as they remain constant to the common usage, as with something merely reproduced by memory" (Paul, 1886, 97–8). In this remark, it is only the reference to "the old science of language" that is subject to qualification. In fact, the realization that this "creative" aspect of language is its essential characteristic can be traced back at least to the seventeenth century. Thus we find the Cartesian view that man alone is more than mere automatism, and that it is the possession of true language that is the primary indicator of this (see Descartes, *Discourse on Method*, Part V), developed by a follower along these lines (Cordemoy, 1668): "if the organs ... had a certain settled order among them [i.e., if man were a 'language-producing engine' such as, for example, an artificial speaking machine, rocks that produce an echo, or, to a confirmed Cartesian like Cordemoy, a parrot], they could never change it, so that when the first voice were heard, those that were wont to follow it would needs be heard also ... whereas the words which I hear utter'd by Bodies, made like mine, have almost never the same sequel" (6) – "to speak, is not to repeat the same words, which have struck the ear, but to utter others to their purpose and suitable to them" (13). In any event, whatever the antiquity of this insight may be, it is clear that a theory of language that neglects this "creative" aspect is of only marginal interest.

On the basis of a limited experience with the data of speech, each normal human has developed for himself a thorough competence

---

sleep furiously", "remorse felt John", "the dog looks barking", etc., are not to be distinguished, in this view, from "revolutionary new ideas appear infrequently", "John felt remorse", "the dog looks frightening", though the distinction can clearly be both stated and motivated on syntactic grounds. Thus grammar reduces to such matters as government, agreement, inflectional paradigms, and the like. This decision seems to me no more defensible than a decision to restrict the study of language structure to phonetic patterning.

in his native language. This competence can be represented, to an as yet undetermined extent, as a system of rules that we can call the *grammar* of his language. To each phonetically possible utterance (cf. § 4.2), the grammar assigns a certain *structural description* that specifies the linguistic elements of which it is constituted and their structural relations (or, in the case of ambiguity, several such structural descriptions). For some utterances, the structural description will indicate, in particular, that they are perfectly well-formed sentences. This set we can call the *language generated by the grammar*. To others, the grammar will assign structural descriptions that indicate the manner of their deviation from perfect well-formedness. Where the deviation is sufficiently limited, an interpretation can often be imposed by virtue of formal relations to sentences of the generated language.

The grammar, then, is a device that (in particular) specifies the infinite set of well-formed sentences and assigns to each of these one or more structural descriptions. Perhaps we should call such a device a *generative grammar* to distinguish it from descriptive statements that merely present the inventory of elements that appear in structural descriptions, and their contextual variants.

The generative grammar of a language should, ideally, contain a central *syntactic component* and two *interpretive components*, a *phonological component* and a *semantic component*. The syntactic component generates strings of minimal syntactically functioning elements (following Bolinger, 1948, let us call them *formatives*) and specifies the categories, functions and structural interrelations of the formatives and systems of formatives. The phonological component converts a string of formatives of specified syntactic structure into a phonetic representation. The semantic component, correspondingly, assigns a semantic interpretation to an abstract structure generated by the syntactic component. Thus each of the two interpretive components maps a syntactically generated structure onto a "concrete" interpretation, in one case phonetic and in the other, semantic. The grammar as a whole can thus be regarded as, ultimately, a device for pairing phonetically represented signals with semantic interpretations, this pairing being mediated through a system of abstract structures generated by the syntactic component. Thus the syntactic component must provide for each sentence (actually, for each interpretation of each sentence) a semantically interpretable *deep structure* and a phonetically interpretable *surface structure*, and, in the event that these are distinct, a statement of the relation between these structures. For further discussion, see Katz and Postal (forthcoming). Roughly speaking, it seems that this much structure is common to all theories of generative grammar, or is at least compatible with them. Beyond this loose and minimal specification, however, important differences emerge.

The generative grammar internalized by someone who has acquired a language defines what in Saussurian terms we may call *langue* (with a qualification to be specified below, on p. 23). In performing as a speaker or hearer, he puts this device to use. Thus as a hearer, his problem is to determine the structural description assigned by his grammar to a presented utterance (or, where the sentence is ambiguous, to determine the correct structural description for this particular token), and using the information in the structural description, to understand the utterance. Clearly the description of intrinsic competence provided by the grammar is not to be confused with an account of actual performance, as de Saussure emphasized with such lucidity (cf. also Sapir, 1921; Newman, 1941). Nor is it to be confused with an account of potential performance.[3] The actual use of language obviously involves a complex interplay of many factors of the most disparate sort, of which the grammatical processes constitute only one. It seems natural to suppose that the study of actual linguistic performance can be seriously pursued only to the extent that we have a good understanding of the generative grammars that are ac-

---

[3]   The common characterization of language as a set of "verbal habits" or as a "complex of present dispositions to verbal behavior, in which speakers of the same language have perforce come to resemble one another" (Quine, 1960, 27) is totally inadequate. Knowledge of one's language is not reflected directly in linguistic habits and dispositions, and it is clear that speakers of the same language or dialect may differ enormously in dispositions to verbal response, depending on personality, beliefs and countless other extra-linguistic factors.

quired by the learner and put to use by the speaker or hearer. The classical Saussurian assumption of the logical priority of the study of *langue* (and, we may add, the generative grammars that describe it) seems quite inescapable.

In the background of the discussion below there will be two conflicting models of generative grammar. The first – which I will call the *taxonomic model* – is a direct outgrowth of modern structural linguistics. The second – which I will call the *transformational model* – is much closer to traditional grammar. It should be noted, however, that modern grammars are typically not conceived as generative grammars, but as descriptive statements about a given corpus (text). Hence the taxonomic model, as described below, is no more than an attempt to formulate a generative grammar which is in the spirit of modern procedural and descriptive approaches. The essential reliance on procedures of segmentation and classification, and on statements of syntagmatic and paradigmatic distribution, is widely shared, however (cf. de Saussure, Hjelmslev, Harris, among others); and these notions clearly suggest a generative grammar with the characteristics of the taxonomic model, as considered here.

The taxonomic model is far simpler, more "concrete" and more "atomistic" than the transformational model. We can characterize it briefly in the following way. Each rule is of the form: the category A has the member (variant, realization) X in the context Z–W. Let us call such a rule a *rewriting rule*. The syntactic component consists of an unordered set of rewriting rules, each of which states the membership of some phrase category or formative category in some context.[4] The structural description that it pro-

---

[4] On the syntactic level, the taxonomic model is a generalization from Harris' morpheme-to-utterance statements, which constitute the nearest approach to an explicit generative grammar on this level. Furthermore, most modern work in syntax is actually more adequately formalized in terms of rewriting rules with null context (i.e., *context-free grammar* – in particular, this seems to be true of Pike's tagmemics, as of most work in IC analysis). Similarly, most, if not all of the work involving use of computers for analysis of sentence structure seems to fall within this narrower framework (cf. Gross, 1962). This is to say that both the sets of sentences generable and, much more importantly, even the systems of structural descriptions generable within the framework of IC analysis seem to

vides can be regarded as a labelled bracketing of the string of formatives, indicating the category of each substring which is a constituent. Let us call such a labelled bracketing, obtainable automatically from a single derivation, a *Phrase-marker* of this string of formatives. The phonological component consists of two distinct sets of rewriting rules. The first set (morphophonemic rules) states the phonemic constitution of morphophonemes or formatives with respect to stated contexts. The second set (phonetic rules) states the phonetic constitution of phonemes, with respect to stated contexts. Each of these sets is unordered.

The transformational model is far more complex and highly structured. In one formulation of this model, the syntactic component is assumed to consist of two subcomponents. The first (constituent structure) subcomponent consists of an ordered set of rewriting rules that generate strings of formatives that we may call *C-terminal strings*. These constitute either a finite set, or a highly restricted infinite set. The second (transformational) sub-

---

be adequately represented by the mechanism of generation of strings and of structural descriptions (Phrase-markers) formalized within this theory (cf. Postal, 1964, in this connection). Though abstract study of such systems is recent, there is already a fairly substantial body of results. Cf. Chomsky (1963), Schützenberger and Chomsky (1963) for summaries of recent work. I do not think that the variations that have been proposed within this general framework have any bearing on the conclusions developed below, regarding the taxonomic model. From the point of view of linguistic adequacy, of course, the important question about a theory of grammar (e.g., the taxonomic model, or the theory of context-free grammar) is not so much the question of the sets of strings that are generable (the *weak generative capacity* of this theory), but rather that of the sets of structural descriptions that are generable within the framework of this theory (its *strong generative capacity*), and, even more important, the question of its explanatory adequacy. It is questions of the latter sort that have, quite naturally, dominated the discussion of linguistic adequacy, and it is such questions that I will consider below. However, it is interesting to observe that several examples are now known of subparts of natural languages that are beyond the weak generative capacity of the theory of context-free grammar (cf. Postal, 1961, 1964; Miller and Chomsky, 1963), Though this is not the linguistically most significant deficiency of this theory, it is sufficient to show that in attempting to enrich the theory of grammar to overcome the inadequacies of such systems, we must not only go beyond them in strong generative capacity and explanatory adequacy, but we must develop a theory that departs from the theory of context-free grammar in weak generative capacity as well.

component consists of a partially ordered set of complex operations called (*grammatical*) *transformations*, each of which maps a full Phrase-marker (or a pair, triple, etc. of Phrase-markers) of some terminal string (or a pair, triple, etc. of terminal strings) into a new *derived Phrase-marker* of a *T-terminal string*. Some of the rewriting and transformational rules may be obligatory, while others are optional. Application of all obligatory and perhaps some optional rules of the syntactic component, observing order, will give a T-terminal string with a derived Phrase-marker. The structural description of this string will be a set of Phrase-markers (one for each underlying C-terminal string, and, in addition, the derived Phrase-marker of the full string) and a representation of its "transformational history", what we may call a *Transformation-marker*. We will see below that all of this information plays a role in determining the full semantic and phonetic interpretation of an utterance.[5] It is also essential to distinguish a *lexicon*, with rather different properties, but I will not go into this question here.

The phonological component of a transformational generative grammar consists of an ordered set of rewriting rules, an ordered set of transformational rules, and an ordered set of rewriting rules, in that order. The transformational rules, furthermore, apply in a cycle, first to the smallest constituents of a string, then to the next largest constituents, etc., until the maximal domain of phonological processes is reached. These are, technically, transformational rules since they involve the constituent structure of the utterance (this is the sense in which the word "transformation" has been used in the study of generative grammar). This *transformational cycle* determines the phonetic form of syntactically complex units from the underlying (abstract) phonemic form of their components,

---

[5] The most accessible summary of formal properties of grammatical transformations, from this point of view, is in Chomsky (1961a). For further details, see Chomsky (1955, chapters 8, 9). The most extensive study of English grammar within this framework is Lees (1960a). See the bibliography of the second printing (1962) of Chomsky (1957a) for references to much recent work. In addition, cf. Schachter (1961, 1962), Postal (1962), Langendoen (1963b).

using the manner of composition specified by the derived Phrase-marker.[6]

Investigation of the semantic component of a transformational grammar is quite recent. It has proceeded from the assumption, implicit in all studies of transformational grammar, that the grammatical functions and relations that play the primary role in determining the semantic interpretation of a sentence are those that are represented (in the manner described in § 4.1, below) in the underlying Phrase-markers generated by the constituent structure subcomponent, so that these Phrase-markers constitute the basic "content elements" underlying the interpretation of actual sentences (cf. Harris, 1957, pp. 290, 339–40; Chomsky, 1957, p. 92). For investigation of the semantic component, in which these vague suggestions are refined, sharpened, and considerably elaborated and developed, see Katz and Fodor (1963); Katz and Postal (forthcoming).

In terms of the characterization of a generative grammar given above (p. 9–10), we can distinguish between the taxonomic and transformational models in the following simple way. The syntactic component of a taxonomic grammar provides a single Phrase-marker for each utterance (in each interpretation) which serves both as deep structure and surface structure. That is, this single labelled bracketing of a formative sequence contains all information relevant to its semantic or phonetic interpretation. In a transformational grammar, the Phrase-markers of the underlying strings and the Transformation-marker constitute, jointly, the deep structure, and contain all information relevant to semantic interpretation; while the labelled bracketing that constitutes the final derived Phrase-marker of the T-terminal string is the surface structure which, presumably, contains all and only the

---

[6] For examples of the operation of the transformational cycle, see Chomsky, Halle, Lukoff (1956); Halle and Chomsky (1960); Halle (1961b, 1963); Miller and Chomsky (1963); Lightner (1963); Bever and Langendoen (1963); Bever (1963); Langendoen (1963b); McCawley (1963); Halle and Zeps (forthcoming). The structure of the phonological component of a transformational grammar, with particular reference to English, is discussed in more detail in Halle and Chomsky (forthcoming).

information relevant to phonetic interpretation. Katz and Postal (forthcoming) have, furthermore, presented strong arguments for the view that singulary transformations make no contribution to semantic interpretation, so that the contribution of the Transformation-marker to the deep structure is minimal. In fact, recent and still unpublished work suggests that it can be entirely eliminated, but I will not pursue this matter further here. The important point is that according to this conception of grammatical structure, the categories and grammatical functions represented in the actual labelled bracketing of the temporally given string will, in general, not be those that determine the semantic interpretation of this string, though they will be directly related to its phonetic interpretation. It is in the system of underlying structures that are mapped onto the actual given string by transformational rules that the semantically significant categories and functions are represented.

The transformational model, so described, expresses a view of the structure of language which is not at all new. In particular, we find the observation that the semantic content of a sentence is represented only in an unexpressed deep structure, based on elementary underlying strings, in the *Grammaire générale et raisonnée* of Port-Royal (1660). Thus the authors discuss the sentence "Dieu invisible a créé le monde visible" (68–69), with complex Subject and Predicate (that is, with phrases rather than simply categories as Subject and Predicate), and observe that its semantic content is expressed in the three underlying judgments that "Dieu est invisible", that "il a créé le monde", and that "le monde est visible", of which the second is "la principale et l'essentielle de la proposition", while the first and third are "incidentes" (in the terminology suggested by Lees, 1960, the second is the *matrix* structure and the first and third, the *constituent* structures). They point out that each of the three underlying structures that represent the semantic content could be converted into a sentence in itself (a *kernel* sentence, in current terminology), but that in general the "propositions incidentes" are simply represented "dans notre esprit, sans être exprimées par des paroles, comme dans l'exemple proposé" (although, "quelquefois aussi on les marque expressément ...

comme quand je réduis le même exemple à ces termes: 'Dieu *qui*
est invisible a créé le monde *qui* est visible.' ''). Other aspects of
sentence structure (e.g., infinitival constructions) are also analyzed
in this transformational framework, which is then still further
elaborated in the Port-Royal *Logic*.

Notice that in the case of the transformational model, the symbols and structures that are manipulated, rewritten and transformed
as a sentence is generated may bear no very direct relation to any
of its concrete subparts, whereas in the case of the taxonomic
model each of the symbols that is rewritten in the generation of a
sentence stands for a category to which some continuous subpart
of this sentence belongs (or category symbol by which it is represented). It is in this sense that the taxonomic model is both
more concrete and more atomistic.

1.1. Before continuing, it is instructive to consider these notions
from the point of view of traditional grammar, as well as that of
classical linguistic theory and of modern taxonomic linguistics.

It would not be inaccurate to regard the transformational model
as a formalization of features implicit in traditional grammars, and
to regard these grammars as inexplicit transformational generative
grammars. The goal of a traditional grammar is to provide its
user with the ability to understand an arbitrary sentence of the
language, and to form and employ it properly on the appropriate
occasion. Thus its goal is (at least) as far-reaching as that of a
generative grammar, as just described. Furthermore, the rich
descriptive apparatus of traditional grammar far exceeds the limits
of the taxonomic model, though it is largely, and perhaps fully
formalizable within the framework of the transformational model.
However, it is important to bear in mind that even the most careful
and complete traditional grammar relies in an essential way on the
intuition and intelligence of the user, who is expected to draw the
correct inferences from the many examples and hints (and explicit
lists of irregularities) presented by the grammar. If the grammar
is a good one, the user may succeed, but the deep-seated regularities
of the language that he somehow discovers escape explicit formu-

lation, and the nature of the abilities that enable him to perform
this task remain a complete mystery. The vastness of these gaps can
be appreciated only when one makes an attempt to construct
explicit rules to account for the full range of structural information
available to the mature user of a language.

Focusing on the notion of "creativity", one can distinguish two
conflicting views regarding the essential nature of language in
Nineteenth Century linguistic theory.

On the one hand, we have the Humboldtian view that "man muss
die *Sprache* nicht sowohl wie ein todtes *Erzeugtes*, sondern weit
mehr wie eine *Erzeugung* ansehen" (1836, § 8, p. LV). The essence
of each language is what Humboldt designates as its characteristic
Form (not to be identified solely with "inner form"). The form of
language is that constant and unvarying factor that underlies and
gives life and significance to each particular new linguistic act. It is
by having developed an internal representation of this form that
each individual is capable of understanding the language and using
it in a way that is intelligible to his fellow speakers. This characteristic form determines and inheres in each separate linguistic element.
The role and significance of each individual element can be determined only by considering it in relation to underlying form, that is,
in relation to the fixed generative rules that determine the manner of
its formation. It is this underlying generative principle that the linguist must seek to represent in a descriptive grammar. The notion
of "form" as "generative process" underlies Humboldt's entire account of the nature of language and of the use and acquisition of
language, and constitutes perhaps his most original and fruitful contribution to linguistic theory.

Cf., for example, such representative passages as these: „Das Verfahren
der Sprache ist aber nicht bloss ein solches, wodurch eine einzelne Er-
scheinung zu Stande kommt; es muss derselben zugleich die Möglich-
keit eröffnen, eine unbestimmbare Menge solcher Erscheinungen, und
unter allen, ihr von dem Gedanken gestellten Bedingungen, hervorzubringen... [die Sprache] muss daher von endlichen Mitteln einen unend-
lichen Gebrauch machen." (§ 13, p. CXXII) „... [die Form] ... ist in ihrer
Natur selbst eine Auffassung der einzelnen, im Gegensatze zu ihr als
Stoff zu betrachtenden, *Sprachelemente* in *geistiger Einheit*. Denn in jeder

Sprache liegt eine solche [Einheit], und durch diese zusammenfassende Einheit macht eine Nation die ihr von ihren Vorfahren überlieferte Sprache zu der ihrigen. Dieselbe Einheit muss sich also in der Darstellung wiederfinden; und nur wenn man von den zerstreuten Elementen bis zu dieser Einheit hinaufsteigt, erhält man wahrhaft einen Begriff von der Sprache selbst, da man, ohne ein solches Verfahren, offenbar Gefahr läuft, nicht einmal jene Elemente in ihrer wahren Eigentümlichkeit, und noch weniger in ihrem realen Zusammenhange zu verstehen" (§ 8, p. LXII). „Es versteht sich indess von selbst, dass in den Begriff der Form der Sprache keine Einzelheit als *isolirte* Thatsache, sondern immer nur insofern aufgenommen werden darf, als sich eine Methode der Sprachbildung an ihr entdecken lässt" (§ 8, p. LXII). „Die charakteristische Form der Sprachen hängt an jedem *einzelnen* ihrer kleinsten Elemente; jedes wird durch sie, wie unerklärlich es im Einzelnen sei, auf irgend eine Weise bestimmt. Dagegen ist es kaum möglich, Punkte aufzufinden, von denen sich behaupten liesse, dass sie an ihnen, einzeln genommen, entscheidend haftete" (§ 8, p. LIX). „Denn die Sprache ist ja nicht als ein daliegender, in seinem Ganzen übersehbarer, oder nach und nach mitteilbarer Stoff, sondern muss als ein sich ewig *erzeugender* angesehen werden, wo die Gesetze der Erzeugung bestimmt sind, aber der Umfang und gewissermassen auch die Art des Erzeugnisses ganzlich unbestimmt bleiben" (§ 9, p. LXXI). „Die Sprache besteht, neben den schon geformten Elementen, ganz vorzüglich auch aus Methoden, die Arbeit des Geistes, welcher sie die Bahn und die Form vorzeichnet, weiter fortzusetzen" (§ 9, p. LXXVII). „Das in dieser Arbeit des Geistes, den articulirten Laut zum Gedankenausdruck zu erheben, liegende Beständige und Gleichförmige, so vollständig, als möglich, in seinem Zusammenhange aufgefasst, und systematisch dargestellt, macht die *Form* der Sprache aus" (§ 8, p. LVIII).

In Humboldt's sense, *Form* extends beyond grammatical form (beyond "Redefügung" and "Wortbildung") to encompass also the substantive characterization of the sound system (§ 8, p. LX) and the principles of concept formation as embodied in the system of stems ("Grundwörter") (§ 8, p. LXI). "Überhaupt wird durch den Begriff Form nichts Factisches und Individuelles ausgeschlossen..." (§ 8, p. LXII).

From this conception of the nature of language, Humboldt derives his views concerning understanding of speech and acquisition of language. Speaking and understanding are, in his view, differing manifestations of the same underlying capacity, the same

generative principle, mastery of which provides the speaker-hearer
with the ability to use and understand all of the infinite range of
linguistic items ("Mit dem *Verstehen* verhält es sich nicht anders.
Es kann in der Seele nichts, als durch eigne Thätigkeit vorhanden
sein, und Verstehen und Sprechen sind nur verschiedenartige
Wirkungen der nämlichen Sprachkraft. Die gemeinsame Rede ist
nie mit dem Übergeben eines Stoffes vergleichbar. In dem Verste-
henden, wie im Sprechenden, muss derselbe aus der eigenen, innern
Kraft entwickelt werden; und was der erstere empfängt, ist nur die
harmonisch stimmende Anregung. Es ist daher dem Menschen
auch schon natürlich, das eben Verstandene wieder gleich auszu-
sprechen. Auf diese Weise liegt die Sprache in jedem Menschen in
ihrem ganzen Umfange, was aber nichts Anderes bedeutet, als
dass jeder ein ... geregeltes Streben besitzt, die ganze Sprache, wie
es äussere oder innere Veranlassung herbeiführt, nach und nach
aus sich hervorzubringen und hervorgebracht zu verstehen" – § 9,
p. LXX). Furthermore, since language consists essentially of a
"System von Regeln" as well as a "Vorrath von Wörtern" – (cf. § 9,
p. LXXVIII), common to speaker and hearer, it follows that "Das
Sprechenlernen der Kinder ist nicht ein Zumessen von Wörtern,
Niederlegen im Gedächtnis, und Wiedernachlallen mit den Lippen,
sondern ein Wachsen des Sprachvermögens durch Alter und Übung"
(§ 9, p. LXXI). "... [Die Sprache] ... lässt sich ..., wenn es auch auf
den ersten Anblick anders erscheint, nicht eigentlich lehren, sondern
nur im Gemüthe wecken; man kann ihr nur den Faden hingeben,
an dem sie sich von selbst entwickelt" (§ 6, p. L). "Die Erlernung
ist ... immer nur Wiedererzeugung" (§ 13, CXXVI).

It is just this point of view concerning the essential nature of
language that underlies and motivates recent work in generative
grammar. Furthermore, the Humboldtian views concerning perception and acquisition have re-emerged, in many particulars, in
the course of this work (cf., e.g., Chomsky, 1957a, 48; 1960; 1961a,
§§ 1,2; and the references of note 23, p. 100). A generative grammar,
in the sense sketched above, is an attempt to represent, in a precise
manner, certain aspects of the *Form* of language, and a particular
theory of generative grammar is an attempt to specify those aspects

of form that are a common human possession – in Humboldtian terms, one might identify this latter with the underlying general form of all language ("Die Formen mehrerer Sprachen können in einer noch allgemeineren Form zusammenkommen, und die Formen aller thun dies in der That, insofern man überall bloss von dem Allgemeinsten ausgeht" ... "dass man ebenso richtig sagen kann, dass das ganze Menschengeschlecht nur Eine Sprache, als das jeder Mensch eine besondere besitzt" – § 8, LXIII). There is one respect (to which we return directly below) in which this work diverges in principle from the Humboldtian framework; beyond this, the narrower limitations within which it has concretely developed (in particular, insofar as very little has been said, until quite recently, concerning semantic or conceptual structure) are a result not of any point of principle, but rather of the fact that there has been little to say about these further matters that could withstand serious analysis (cf. § 2.3).

Humboldt's thoughts concerning the semantic aspect of linguistic form are, not surprisingly, rather obscure in certain respects. They are, however, original and suggestive and, in part, quite different from more recent and familiar views. I will only attempt a brief sketch, largely in paraphrase, of what seem to be their main outlines. For Humboldt, as for many others before and since, a word does not stand directly for a thing, but rather for a concept. There can, accordingly, be a multiplicity of expressions for the same object, each representing a way in which this object has been conceived through the workings of the process of "Spracherzeugung", and Humboldt gives several Sanskrit examples, of the now familiar "morning star" – "evening star" type, to illustrate this (§ 11). The process of language formation is, furthermore, constantly active. Thus, one cannot regard the lexicon of a language as a completed aggregate ("eine fertig daliegende Masse"), but rather only as "ein fortgehendes Erzeugnis und Wiedererzeugnis des wortbildenden Vermögens" (§ 13). This is to say that the capacity of "Spracherzeugung" is constantly at work, not only in extending the system of concepts, but also in recreating it, in each perceptual act (thus memory limitations are overcome, since the system of concepts is not stored in full detail, but only in terms of its "generating principle"). In two respects, then, a system of concepts is not to be regarded as constituting a store of well-defined objects (as, apparently, it is for Saussure). In particular, even with the system fixed, Humboldt denies that understanding a linguistic expression is simply a matter of selecting the fully specified concept from a "store of concepts". It is rather that the received signs activate within the listener a corresponding link in his system of concepts ("dass sie gegenseitig in einander dasselbe Glied der Kette ihrer sinnlichen Vorstellungen und inneren Begriffserzeugungen berühren", § 20, CCXIII), causing a corresponding, but not identical concept to emerge. When a "key of the mental instrument" is touched in this way, the whole system will resonate, and the emerging concept will stand in harmony with all that surrounds it to the most remote regions of its domain. Thus, a system of concepts is activated in the listener, and it is the place of a concept within this system (which may differ somewhat from speaker to speaker) that, in part, determines the way in which the hearer understands a linguistic expression. Finally, the concepts so formed are systematically interrelated in an "inner totality", with varying interconnections and structural relations (§ 20). This inner totality, formed by the use of language in thought, conception, and expression of feeling, functions as a conceptual world interposed through the constant activity of the mind between itself and the actual objects, and it is within this system that a word obtains its value ("Geltung" – cf. Saussure). Consequently, a language should not be regarded merely, or primarily, as a means of communication (Austauschungsmittel), and the instrumental use of language (its use for achieving concrete aims) is derivative and subsidiary. It is, for Humboldt, typical only of parasitic systems (e.g., "Sprachmischungen", as the lingua franca along the Mediterranean coast.)

For further discussion of Humboldtian general linguistics, see Viertel (forthcoming).

In sharp contrast to the Humboldtian conception, in the general linguistics of the Nineteenth Century, is the view that is perhaps expressed most clearly by Whitney (1872); namely, that "language in the concrete sense ... [is] ... the sum of words and phrases by which any man expresses his thought" (372); that study of speech is no more than study of a body of vocal signs; and that study of the origin and development of language is nothing more than study of origin and development of these signs. The problem of accounting for the acquisition of language, so conceived, disappears. "... the acquisition of language by children does not seem to us any mystery at all." It is not at all astonishing "that a child, after hearing a certain word used some scores or hundreds of times, comes to understand what it means, and then, a little later, to pronounce and use it ...".

This narrowing of the scope of linguistics to the study of inventory of elements was occasioned not only by the dramatic successes of comparative linguistics, which operated within these limitations, but also by the unclarities and obscurities of formulation of Humboldt ("a man whom it is nowadays the fashion to praise highly, without understanding or even reading him" – Whitney, 1872, 333) and his successors. Furthermore, there were some serious confusions concerning the notion of "creativity". Thus it is significant that the comments of Paul's quoted above are from a chapter that deals with analogic change. He makes no distinction (just as Humboldt makes no clear distinction) between the kind of "creativity" that leaves the language entirely unchanged (as in the production – and understanding – of new sentences, an activity in which the adult is constantly engaged) and the kind that actually changes the set of grammatical rules (e.g., analogic change). But this is a fundamental distinction. In fact, the technical tools for dealing with "rule-governed creativity," as distinct from "rule-changing creativity", have become readily available only during the past few decades in the course of work in logic and foundations of mathematics. But in the light of these developments, it is possible to return to the questions to which Humboldt addressed himself, and to attempt to represent certain aspects of the underlying "Form of language", insofar as it encompasses "rule-governed creativity", by means of an explicit generative grammar.

Saussure, like Whitney (and possibly under his influence – cf. Godel, 1957, 32-3), regards *langue* as basically a store of signs with their grammatical properties, that is, a store of word-like elements, fixed phrases and, perhaps, certain limited phrase types (though it is possible that his rather obscure concept of "mécanisme de la langue" was intended to go beyond this – cf. Godel, 1957, 250). He was thus quite unable to come to grips with the recursive processes underlying sentence formation, and he appears to regard sentence formation as a matter of *parole* rather than *langue*, of free and voluntary creation rather than systematic rule (or perhaps, in some obscure way, as on the border between *langue* and *parole*). There is no place in his scheme for "rule-governed creativity" of the kind involved in the ordinary everyday use of language. At the same time, the influence of Humboldtian holism (but now restricted to inventories and paradigmatic sets, rather than to the full-scale generative processes that constitute *Form*) is apparent in the central role of the notions "terme" and "valeur" in the Saussurian system.

Modern linguistics is much under the influence of Saussure's conception of *langue* as an inventory of elements (Saussure, 1916, 154, and elsewhere, frequently) and his preoccupation with systems of elements rather than the systems of rules which were the focus of attention in traditional grammar and in the general linguistics of Humboldt. In general, modern descriptive statements pay little attention to the "creative" aspect of language; they do not face the problem of presenting the system of generative rules that assign structural descriptions to arbitrary utterances and thus embody the speaker's competence in and knowledge of his language. Furthermore, this narrowing of the range of interest, as compared with traditional grammar, apparently has the effect of making it impossible to select an inventory of elements correctly, since it seems that no inventory (not even that of phonemes) can be determined without reference to the principles by which sentences are constructed in the language (cf. § 4.3–5). To the extent that this is true, "structural linguistics" will have suffered from a failure to appreciate the extent and depth of interconnections among various parts of a language system. By a rather arbitrary limitation of scope, modern linguistics may well have become engaged in an intensive study of mere artifacts. We return to this matter below. In summary, a comparison of Humboldtian general linguistics with typical modern views reveals quite a number of basic differences. Thus Humboldt's belief that the instrumental function of language is derivative, and that it is the characteristic property only of parasitic special purpose systems, contrasts with the view of, for example, Bloomfield (1933, p. 22f.) and Wittgenstein (1958, p. 16–17) that this instrumental function is paradigmatic and basic, and that (for Wittgenstein) its study "is the study of primitive forms of language or primitive languages". Furthermore, Humboldt's conception of underlying form as a system of generative rules that defines the role of each element differentiates his approach strikingly from that of modern structural linguistics, with its emphasis on element and inventory. In the same vein, one may compare his account of how a rich system of generative principles is involved in understanding a particular utterance with the late view of Wittgenstein (1958, p. 42) that there is no necessity to suppose the whole "calculus of language" to be present to the mind as a permanent background for each act of language use. Correspondingly, Humboldt's account of perception in terms of a schematism involving a system of rules contrasts with the elementary data-processing approach characteristic of modern linguistic theory (cf. sections 4, 5, below). Finally, it is interesting to compare Humboldt's views on language-learning (which might, with certain reservations, be called "Platonistic"; cf., in this connection, Leibniz, *Discourse on metaphysics*, section 26) with the typical modern notion expressed, for example, in Wittgenstein's claim (1958, p. 1f., 12–3, 27) that the meanings of words must not only be learned, but also taught (the only means being drill, explanation, or the supplying of rules that are used consciously and explicitly), or in the claim (cf., e.g., Quine, 1960, p. 9f.) that sentences are, typically, "learned" by some sort of process of stimulus-sentence conditioning or sentence-sentence association (with analogic extension of some elementary sort playing a marginal, and in principle dispensable role).

These rather random remarks and examples suggest that it might be instructive to delineate more precisely a "Humboldtian" and a "taxonomic-behaviorist" point of view concerning the nature of language, and to contrast the approaches to language use and acquisition to which these conflicting viewpoints give rise. I think it is historically accurate to regard the approach presented in this paper as basically Humboldtian in its assumption that serious investigation of language use and acquisition presupposes a study of underlying generative processes (for which, to be sure, actual performance will supply evidence), and that very little is to be expected of direct operational analysis of "mentalistic" terms or radical behaviorist reductionism of the sort that has been so dominant in modern speculation on language and cognition. Clarification and justification of this remark is an undertaking that goes well beyond the scope of this paper. I can do no more here than indicate certain points of contact between Humboldtian general linguistics, on the one hand, and recent work on generative grammar and its implications, on the other.

It is, incidentally, interesting to take note of a curious and rather extreme contemporary view to the effect that true linguistic science must *necessarily* be a kind of pre-Darwinian taxonomy concerned solely with the collection and classification of countless specimens, while any attempt to formulate underlying principles and to concentrate on the kinds of data that shed some light on these is taken to be some novel sort of "engineering".[7] Perhaps this notion, which seems to me to defy comment, is related to the equally strange and factually quite incorrect view (recently expressed, e.g., by Joos, 1961; Reichling, 1961; Mel'chuk, 1961; Juilliand, 1961) that current work in generative grammar is in some way an outgrowth of attempts to use electronic computers for one or another purpose, whereas in fact it should be obvious that its roots are firmly in traditional linguistics.

1.2. The issues involved can be clarified by setting linguistic theory

---

[7] See Bolinger (1960) for an elaboration of this point of view. See also the Introduction to Joos (1957).

LIBRARY ST. MARY'S COLLEGE

within the general framework of the study of human intellectual capacities and their specific character. Still remaining within the classical framework, as modified above, we can take as an objective for linguistic theory the precise specification of two kinds of abstract device, the first serving as a perceptual model and the second, as a model for acquisition of language.

(1)   (a) utterance $\longrightarrow$ $\boxed{A}$ $\longrightarrow$ structural description

     (b) primary linguistic data $\longrightarrow$ $\boxed{B}$ $\longrightarrow$ generative grammar

The perceptual model A is a device that assigns a full structural description D to a presented utterance U, utilizing in the process its internalized generative grammar G, where G generates a phonetic representation R of U with the structural description D. In Saussurian terms, U is a specimen of *parole* interpreted by the device A as a "performance" of the item R which has the structural description D and which belongs to the *langue* generated by G. The learning model B is a device which constructs a theory G (i.e., a generative grammar G of a certain *langue*) as its output, on the basis of primary linguistic data (e.g., specimens of *parole*), as input. To perform this task, it utilizes its given *faculté de langage*, its innate specification of certain heuristic procedures and certain built-in constraints on the character of the task to be performed. We can think of general linguistic theory as an attempt to specify the character of the device B. We can regard a particular grammar as, in part, an attempt to specify the information available in principle (i.e., apart from limitations of attention, memory, etc.) to A that makes it capable of understanding an arbitrary utterance, to the highly non-trivial extent that understanding is determined by the structural description provided by the generative grammar. In evaluating a particular generative grammar, we ask whether the information that it gives us about a language is correct, that is, whether it describes correctly the linguistic intuition of the speaker (Saussure's "conscience des sujets parlants", which to him, as to Sapir, provides the ultimate test of adequacy for a linguistic description). In evaluating a general theory of linguistic structure that is sufficiently explicit to offer an actual hypothesis about the character of B, we ask whether the generative grammars that it selects meet the empirical criterion of correspondence to the speaker's linguistic intuition, in the case of particular languages.

I will try to show that the taxonomic model (or any of its variants within modern study of language) is far too oversimplified to be able to account for the facts of linguistic structure and that the transformational model of generative grammar is much closer to the truth. To show that modern linguistics seriously underestimates the richness of structure of language and the generative processes that underlie it, it is necessary to sample the range of problems that cannot be attacked, or often even posed within the narrow limits that it sets. A variety of examples of this sort will be considered in the following sections. I will also try to show that these inadequacies and limitations may in part be traceable to an impoverished conception of the nature of human cognitive processes, and that a return to traditional concerns and viewpoints, with the higher standards of explicitness that have emerged in modern linguistics, can perhaps provide new insights concerning perception and learning.

2

LEVELS OF SUCCESS FOR GRAMMATICAL
DESCRIPTION

2.0. Within the framework outlined above, we can sketch various levels of success that might be attained by a grammatical description associated with a particular linguistic theory. The lowest level of success is achieved if the grammar presents the observed primary data correctly.[1] A second and higher level of success is achieved when the grammar gives a correct account of the linguistic intuition of the native speaker, and specifies the observed data (in particular) in terms of significant generalizations that express underlying regularities in the language. A third and still higher level of success is achieved when the associated linguistic theory provides a general basis for selecting a grammar that achieves the second level of success over other grammars consistent with the relevant observed data that do not achieve this level of success. In this case, we can say that the linguistic theory in question suggests an explanation for the linguistic intuition of the native speaker. It can be interpreted as asserting that data of the observed kind will enable a speaker whose intrinsic capacities are as represented in this general theory to construct for himself a grammar that characterizes exactly this linguistic intuition.

[1] Innocuous as this comment may seem, it still requires qualification. What data is relevant is determined in part by the possibility for a systematic theory, and one might therefore hold that the lowest level of success is no easier to achieve than the others. As noted above, the fact that a certain noise was produced, even intentionally, by an English speaker does not guarantee that it is a well-formed specimen of his language. Under many circumstances it is quite appropriate to use deviant utterances. Furthermore, under normal conditions speech is subject to various, often violent distortions that may in themselves indicate nothing about the underlying linguistic patterns. The problem of determining what data is valuable and to the point is not an easy one. What is observed is often neither relevant nor significant, and what is relevant and significant is often very difficult to observe, in linguistics no less than in the freshman physics laboratory, or, for that matter, anywhere in science.

For later reference, let us refer to these roughly delimited levels of success as the levels of *observational adequacy, descriptive adequacy*, and *explanatory adequacy*, respectively. In terms of the notions of the preceding section, a grammar that aims for observational adequacy is concerned merely to give an account of the primary data (e.g., the corpus) that is the input to the acquisition device (1b); a grammar that aims for descriptive adequacy is concerned to give a correct account of the linguistic intuition of the native speaker; in other words, it is concerned with the output of the device (1b); and a linguistic theory that aims for explanatory adequacy is concerned with the internal structure of the device (1b); that is, it aims to provide a principled basis, independent of any particular language, for the selection of the descriptively adequate grammar of each language.

Modern linguistics has been largely concerned with observational adequacy. In particular, this is true of post-Bloomfieldian American linguistics (cf. below, § 4.3–4), and apparently, of the London school of Firth, with its emphasis on the ad hoc character of linguistic description.[2] Traditional grammar, on the other hand, was explicitly concerned with the level of descriptive adequacy (and this interest persists, explicitly, in Sapir's work, as well as in current work in the traditional mold – cf. Sapir, 1933; Long, 1960). This difference between traditional and modern points of view is made particularly clear in modern critique of traditional grammars. Thus Nida, in his valuable study (1943) of English syntax within the immediate constituent framework, criticizes Jespersen sharply for his "serious distortion and complication of the formal and functional values" in assigning to "the doctor's arrival", but not "the doctor's house", a structural description that indicates that the Subject-Verb relation appears in the former but not in the latter phrase. But clearly Jespersen's account is correct on the level of descriptive adequacy, and the fact that the data-processing operations of modern linguistics fail to provide the correct information indicates only that they are based on an erroneous conception of linguistic structure, or that observational adequacy is

[2]   Cf. Firth et al. (1957).

being taken as the only relevant concern.[3] On the other hand, Jakobson's attempts to formulate universal phonological laws (cf. § 4.2, below) might perhaps be regarded as indicating a concern for explanatory adequacy, on at least one level of grammar. It is clear that the question of explanatory adequacy can be seriously raised only when we are presented with an explicit theory of generative grammar that specifies the form of grammars and suggests a mechanism for selecting among them (i.e., an evaluation procedure for grammars of a specified form). The difference between observational and descriptive adequacy is related to the distinction drawn by Hockett (1958) between "surface grammar" and "deep grammar", and he is unquestionably correct in noting that modern linguistics is largely confined in scope to the former.

2.1. LEVELS OF ADEQUACY IN PHONOLOGY

A few linguistic examples may help to clarify the distinction between these various levels of adequacy. Consider first the case of so-called "accidental gaps" in the lexicon. Thus in English there is a word "pick" /pik/, but no /blik/ or /ftik/. The level of observational adequacy would be attained by a grammar that contained the rule: N → /pik/, but no lexical rule introducing /blik/ or /ftik/. To attain the level of descriptive adequacy, a grammar would have to provide, in addition, a general rule that sets up a specific barrier against /ftik/, but not against /blik/ (which would thus qualify as an accidental gap, a phonologically permissible nonsense syllable). This level would be achieved by a grammar that contained the generalization that in initial position before a true consonant (a segment which is consonantal and nonvocalic, in terms of Jakobson's distinctive features), a consonant is necessarily /s/. The level

---

[3] Nida also criticizes Jespersen, on essentially the same grounds, for describing "barking" in "the barking dogs" as an attributive of the same rank as "barks" in "the dog barks". Again Jespersen's decision seems to me unquestionably correct from the point of view of descriptive adequacy, though internally unmotivated (i.e., deficient from the point of view of explanatory adequacy).

of explanatory adequacy would be attained by a linguistic theory that provides a principled reason for incorporating this generalization in a grammar of English, and for excluding the (factually correct) "rule" that in the context #b-ik a liquid is necessarily /r/. Thus the theory might provide a general evaluation measure (simplicity measure) which would show how the former, but not the latter rule gives a more highly valued grammar. Such a theory would suggest an explanation for the linguistic intuition that /blik/, but not /ftik/, is a "possible" word, though neither has been heard. This is the intuition that would result from observation of actual utterances by a learner who constructs the most highly valued grammar of the appropriate form, as specified by this theory.[4]

Consider now the matter of predictable phonetic variants. Thus in my speech, the lexical item "telegraph" appears in many phonetic shapes, depending on context, in particular, the shapes (2i-iii) in the contexts #—#, -ic-, -y, respectively:

(2) (i) téligrǽf
    (ii) tèligrǽf
    (iii) tilégrif.

Observational adequacy would be achieved by a grammar that

---

[4] The theory of "morpheme structure rules" developed in Halle (1959a, 1959b) constitutes an attempt to reach the level of explanatory adequacy, in this case. Halle shows how consistent adherence to the principle of minimizing feature specifications in the phonological component provides a principled basis for the distinction between accidental and non-accidental gaps. To my knowledge, this is the only attempt to provide a general basis for this distinction, though lists and charts that state much of the data that is to be explained have frequently appeared.

In his review of Halle (1959b), Ferguson (1962, 292) describes Halle's discovery of the role of "morpheme structure rules" as "a misfortune" not too different from certain defects of taxonomic grammars that Halle exposes (cf. § 4.3, below). This is an extremely peculiar conclusion. No generalization is lost by distinguishing morpheme structure rules (which are obviously needed in a full grammar, and which, as Halle shows, play a distinctive role in accounting for an otherwise unexplained area of linguistic fact) from other phonetic rules differing from them both in formal properties and in the phenomena that they describe. On the other hand, the deficiency of taxonomic grammars to which Ferguson alludes involves their inability to state certain generalizations, that is, their inability to achieve descriptive adequacy.

merely states the facts, as I have just done, thus reproducing the observed data in a convenient arrangement. Such a grammar (called, technically, an *item-and-arrangement grammar*) in effect treats the item "telegraph" as an exception, exactly as it treats "see"- "saw", "man" – "men", etc. Thus the grammar would be no more complex if the facts were, instead, that (2i) appears in the context -ic, (2ii) in the context $\# - \#$, and (2iii) in the context -y, the rest of the language remaining fixed. Within this framework, there are no further questions to be raised, and there is nothing more to be said.

To achieve the level of descriptive adequacy, in this case, a grammar must treat the variation of "telegraph" as a special case of general rules applying as well to many other items. It must be able to account for the fact that the phonetic variation of "telegraph" is obviously not capricious, given the rest of English, as is the variation of "man". Not having heard the form "men", it is impossible for the linguist or learner to predict it. But this is not true in the case of (2).

The grammar with its associated linguistic theory would achieve the still higher level of explanatory adequacy, in this case, if this linguistic theory were to provide a framework for phonological rules and an evaluation measure meeting the following condition: the most highly valued system of rules of the appropriate form selected to generate a set of items from which the variants of "telegraph" are excluded would be the system of rules that in fact predicts this contextual variation for "telegraph". In this case, the linguistic theory would provide a basis for explaining the facts presented in (2), in terms of other aspects of English and certain assumptions about the general character of grammars. It would make clear, in other words, the respect in which the actual contextual variation differs from the alternative mentioned in the paragraph following (2). The latter would lead to a less-highly valued grammar – it would not be predicted by the highest-valued grammar based on data that excludes (2). The theory of item-and-arrangement grammar obviously cannot meet this condition, and for this reason (which, clearly, generalizes to a host of similar examples)

cannot be regarded seriously as a theory of grammar.[5] In such cases
as this, neither the level of descriptive nor explanatory adequacy is
easy to obtain, and it is a fact worth considering that despite the
extensive investigations of English phonology in recent years, no
attempt has even been made to reach them.

The point becomes even clearer when we consider phonetic
variants that are syntactically conditioned. Thus English "tórrent"
/tɔrent/ (cf. "torrential") has the reduced vowel [ɨ] in the second
syllable, while the noun "tórment" /tɔrment/ retains the vowel [e].
The level of observational adequacy is attained by the preceding
sentence. The level of descriptive adequacy would be achieved by a
description that managed to relate these observations to the fact
that there is a verb "tormént" but no verb "torrent" in English, by
means of general rules about stress shifts in nouns derived from
verbs ("pérmit", "permít", etc.), and about the role of stress in
preventing vowel reduction. The level of explanatory adequacy
requires a phonological theory that prescribes the general form of
such syntactically determined phonetic processes, and that shows
how the appropriate generalizations, in this case, would appear in
the highest-valued grammar of the prescribed form, even if the
items in question were not part of the observed data from which
this grammar is constructed. Similarly, in the case of such familiar
examples as "light house keeper" (with stress patterns 132, 213, 313),
the level of descriptive adequacy requires, beyond a statement of
these facts, a general account of the rules by which such stress
patterns are assigned in syntactic constructions, and the level of
explanatory adequacy will be achieved only when a general theory
of such processes is forthcoming. It is examples of this sort that
provide the motivation for the transformational cycle of the phonological component, since in these cases the phonetic shape of the
full phrase is determined by that of its constituents. Cf. p. 13, above.

---

[5] See the references of the preceding footnote, and also Chomsky (1959,
1962b), Miller and Chomsky (1963), for discussion of the problem of deve-
loping a phonological theory that meets this condition, for such cases.

2.2. LEVELS OF ADEQUACY IN SYNTAX

Consider next a few syntactic examples. Suppose that the sentences

(3) John is easy to please
(4) John is eager to please

are observed and accepted as well-formed. A grammar that achieves only the level of observational adequacy would, again, merely note this fact in one way or another (e.g., by setting up appropriate lists). To achieve the level of descriptive adequacy, however, a grammar would have to assign structural descriptions indicating that *John* in (3) is the direct object of *please* (the words are grammatically related as in "This pleases John"), while in (4) it is the logical subject of *please* (as in "John pleases someone"). A theory of grammar that does not allow structural descriptions of this sort cannot achieve the level of descriptive adequacy. In cases of this sort, the taxonomic model of generative grammar discussed above (or any of its variants) cannot achieve the level of descriptive adequacy, since information of this kind cannot be represented in the Phrase-marker that it provides as the full structural description on the syntactic level. The transformational model does, however, make grammars available that can supply structural information of this sort, and therefore can, in this case at least, achieve the level of descriptive adequacy. In § 4.1 we will return to the problem of assigning to (3), (4) structural descriptions that provide the full range of syntactic information.

How might a transformational grammar achieve the level of explanatory adequacy in such a case as this? To achieve this level, the theory must provide for the selection of a descriptively adequate grammar, given such data as (3), (4), "John's eagerness (*easiness) to please...", "to please John is easy (*eager)", "John is an easy (*eager) fellow to please", "it pleases John", "John pleases everyone", "John is easy (eager) for us to please", it is easy (*eager) to please John", "John is a person who (it) is easy to please", "this room is not easy to work in (to do decent work in)", "he is easy to do business with", "This knife is very difficult to cut (meat) with", "a hotel lobby is difficult (a difficult place) to meet people in", "he is not easy to get information from", "such flattery is easy to be fooled by" and many other similar and related structures.

The general theory, in other words, would have to make possible the formulation of the underlying generalizations that account for this arrangement of empirical data, and to distinguish these real generalizations from pseudosimplifications that have no lin-- guistic significance. In so doing, the theory would suggest an explanation for the linguistic intuition of native speakers as regards (3) and (4). This explanation would rest on the assumption that the concepts of grammatical structure and "significant generalization" made explicit in this theory constitute the set of tools used by the learner in constructing an internal representation of his language (i.e., a generative grammar), on the basis of presented linguistic data. There is fairly good reason to believe that in the case of (3), (4), the theory of transformational grammar can approach the level of explanatory adequacy, providing a partial explanation for the speaker's linguistic intuition.[6] That is, the grammar that assigns the correct structural descriptions contains generalizations that are not expressed in grammars that fail to provide the correct structural descriptions, and is thus higher-valued, in a sense which can apparently be made precise without much difficulty.

As a second syntactic example, consider the following arrangement of sentences and non-sentences: ("John found the book" – "John was a farmer"), ("the book was found by John" – *"a farmer was been by John"), "(did John) find the book?" *"did John be a farmer?"), (*"found John the book?" – "was John a farmer?"), ("John didn't find the book" – *"John didn't be a farmer"), (*"John foundn't the book" – "John wasn't a farmer"), ("John DID find the book" – *"John DID be a farmer"), ("Bill found the book and so did John" – *"Bill was a farmer and so did John"),

---

[6] See Miller and Chomsky (1963). Cf. also Lees (1960b) for detailed discussion of a class of similar cases. For discussion of measures of evaluation that select grammars with significant generalizations over those that do not contain such generalizations, cf. Chomsky (1955, chapter 3; 1962); Halle (1961a); Halle and Chomsky (forthcoming).

(*"Bill found the book and so found John" – "Bill was a farmer and so was John"), etc. In short, as is well-known, there are a variety of respects, of which these are a sample, in which "be" behaves quite differently from "find". Similarly, "be", but not "find", is an Auxiliary. Traditional grammars merely list these facts as anomalous, and make no attempt to relate them. It can easily be shown, however, that a transformational grammar with a constituent structure subcomponent containing the rules:

(5) (i) $VP \rightarrow Aux + VP_1$
     (ii) $Aux \rightarrow Aux_1 (Aux_2)$
     (iii) $Aux_1 \rightarrow Tense (Modal)$
     (iv) $Aux_2 \rightarrow (have + en) (be + ing)$
     (v) $VP_1 \rightarrow \begin{cases} Verb + NP \\ be + Predicate \end{cases}$

(an analysis which has many independent motivations) will automatically provide for just this range of phenomena, thus reducing a mass of apparent idiosyncracies to underlying regularity (cf. Chomsky, 1955, chapter 7,9; 1957a). In fact, a transformational grammar would have to be complicated considerably to generate the excluded sentences. Here again, then, it seems that the level of explanatory adequacy can be met by a transformational grammar and the theory associated with it.[7]

---

[7]   The well-known (and different) apparent anomalies of "have" are also largely accounted for by (5) and the rules for forming questions, negations, etc. Notice that from these facts one is led to the conclusion that "be", the modals and the auxiliary "have" are not Verbs, in contrast to the familiar treatment of these items as "defective verbs" (cf., e.g., Bloomfield, 1933, 223; or Austin, 1956, who discusses the fact that modals have no progressive or participial forms, and compares them in this respect to "know", etc. – actually, there is no more reason to con.ment on the lack of "to-", "-ing", or "-en" forms of modals than on the fact that nouns do not appear in these positions). Notice also that there is no optional rule of the grammar that allows one to select "be" (though there is an optional rule that allows one to select "be + Predicate"). In this respect, "be" is quite different from most formatives. In general, it seems reasonable to regard an item as meaning-bearing just in case selection of it is subject to an optional rule (thus most formatives are meaning-bearing, as are optional transformations and constructions given by rewriting rules, but not, e.g., phonemes). Where the grammar provides for an optional choice, it makes sense to

A similar problem is posed by certain English compaiative constructions. We have such sentences as "John received a warmer welcome than Bill", "John is a kinder person than Bill", and "John knows a kinder person than Bill", where only the last is ambiguous ("than Bill is", "than Bill does"). Furthermore, although we can have such sentences as "Bill bought a bigger house than John did", "Mary has a bigger red balloon than John", we do not have "Bill bought the bigger house than John did", "Mary has a red bigger balloon than John", "Mary has a bigger redder balloon than John than Bill", etc. At the level of observational adequacy, a grammar might simply state a variety of facts of this kind. But we can in fact reach a higher level of adequacy in this case. Suppose that we have a transformational grammar of English constructed so as to generate in the most economical way the full range of adjectival constructions, excluding comparatives. It can be shown (cf. Smith, 1961) that a large variety of constructions involving comparatives will be generated automatically by the grammar, with the right arrangement of ambiguities, instances and apparent "exceptions", if we add to this grammar, at the appropriate point in the sequence of ordered rules, the generalized transformation that forms the simplest comparative constructions (namely, those of the foim "John is taller than Bill (is)" from "John is tall", "Bill is tall"). Here, then, is an interesting case where it seems proper to say that the general theory of transformational grammar provides an explanation for a complex array of superficially quite disordered data.

The possibilities for attaining higher levels of adequacy, and the difficulties that attend this project, are well illustrated by the problem of formulating in a precise way the rules for construction of relative clauses and interrogatives. These are related operations; a roughly adequate description would be the following. In each terminal string, zero or more Noun Phrases are assigned as a

---

search for the conditions under which it is appropriate to make this choice (this being one aspect of the study of meaning). Thus it would seem reasonable to inquire into the meaning of "Predication" (i.e., choice of "be + Predicate" in rule (5iii)), but not into the meaning of "be", which is no more subject to independent choice than are its particular variants or their individual phonemes.

marker the element *Wh*. To a string containing the Noun Phrase *Wh*+X we may now apply the transformation

(6) Y – *Wh*+X – Z ⟹ *Wh*+X – Y – Z.

Thus from the string "John admires *Wh*+someone", we can form, by (6), the string "*Wh*+someone John admires" (where Z, in this case, is null). The result of (6) is now subject to either the operation of Relativization, which embeds it in the Noun Phrase of a matrix sentence (giving e.g., "he met someone *Wh*+someone John admires") or the operation of *Auxiliary Attraction* which brings the first part of the Auxiliary to the position following *Wh*+X (giving "*Wh*+someone does John admire"). Finally, the resulting string is subject to obligatory rules that replace *Wh*+X by "who", "what", etc. (giving "he met someone who John admires", "who does John admire").[8] Clearly Relativization can be applied only if the Noun of the phrase *Wh*+X is the same as that of the Noun Phrase in which it is embedded. If the string resulting from the operations just described still contains *Wh*-forms which do not introduce relative clauses (i.e., do not refer to a Noun which actually appears in the sentence in a designated position), then this string is an interrogative, and is to be answered by specification of the Noun Phrases that occupy the positions of these *Wh*-forms. Thus we may have such interrogatives as "who admires John?" (in which Auxiliary attraction has applied vacuously), "who(m) does John admire?", "who admires who(m)?", "he met someone who admires who(m)?", "he met someone who(m) who admires?", etc.

---

[8] More details are given in various places, for example, Chomsky (1957, 1962), Lees (1960). The formulation just outlined is suggested by remarks of E. S. Klima. Other sorts of questions can be described in essentially the same way, even yes-or-no questions (as is pointed out in Katz and Postal, forthcoming). It is hardly necessary to warn the reader of the informality of these descriptions. Notice in particular that throughout this discussion, where sentences are said to be "derived from other sentences by transformation," what should be understood is that the abstract forms (categorized terminal strings) underlying them are derived from abstract forms underlying these other sentences. Notice also that such rules as (6) should be regarded as constituting not a transformation, but rather a family of transformations, in the sense of Chomsky (1955, chapter 8), the kth member of which takes the kth analysis of a string that meets the structural condition and performs the specified operation.

Details aside, this much seems fairly clear and can be formalized without difficulty within the framework of transformational grammar. When we investigate the matter more carefully, however, we find that certain additional conditions are necessary for descriptive adequacy. In particular, a closer analysis of American English shows that interrogatives which delete a Noun Phrase can be formed only from singular indefinite Noun Phrases (although relatives and nondeleting interrogatives are not subject to this restriction; thus, "the boys who are in the room," "which boys are in the room?", etc., are perfectly natural). We have such sentences as "you know a boy with (who has) a scar," "you know the boy with (who has) the scar", "who do you know with (who has) a scar?", "I know a boy who was expelled", "who do I know who was expelled?", "who is likely to come to the lecture tonight?", etc. (notice, incidentally, that though such questions are singular in form, they are neutral as to number in meaning – thus there is, in the last example, no implication that only one person is expected). On the other hand, such sentences as "you know a boy with (who has) the scar", "who do you know with (who has) the scar?", "who do I know who were expelled?", "who are likely to come to the lecture tonight?", etc., are all somewhat unnatural. A still closer analysis shows that the distribution of natural and deviant interrogatives mirrors quite closely that of natural and deviant declaratives with singular indefinite *unspecified* Noun Phrases of the form "someone X", "something X", or their variants. Thus the sentences "he found something of yours", "what did he find of yours?", "he found someone else", "who else did he find?", and so on, are perfectly natural, whereas, in contrast, the parallel sentences "he found someone of yours", "who did he find of yours?", "he found a boy else", and so on, are either outright impossible or else highly unnatural. (Notice, however, that we can have "he found a friend of yours", etc., so that there is no simple explanation for this unnaturalness on semantic grounds.) Similarly, we have such phrases as "someone's book", "whose book"; but "something's cover", "what's cover" are both unnatural (though, once again, we find "its cover" alongside of "his book"). Notice also that the sentences "I found a place (in which, where) we can hide the gift", "I found something in which we can hide the gift" are quite natural, although "I found something where we can hide the gift" is not. Correspondingly, we have the interrogative "what did you find in which we can hide the gift?", but not "what did you find where we can hide the gift?" (the only natural interpretation for the latter is quite different, namely, as a paraphrase of "what did you find in the place in which we can hide the gift?"). Notice finally that a certain "semantic gap" in the usage of indefinites is mirrored in interrogatives. Thus "someone" is referentially restricted to humans, and, in many contexts, use of "something" is natural only with reference to inanimate objects, so that there is, in these contexts, no natural way to refer to an unspecified animal. And, in fact, the unnaturalness of such sentences as "I watched something eating its dinner", with reference to a cat, is carried over for the corresponding interrogatives "what is eating its dinner? (the cat or the dog?)," and so on.

Such examples indicate that for the formation of interrogatives, the transformation (6) must be limited to strings of the form Y – $Wh+some+(one, thing)+X - Z$ (where the element $Wh+some+(one, thing)+X$ is a Noun Phrase), although it is free from this restriction when used to form relative clauses (or nondeleting interrogatives). Equivalently, we may say that the Relativization transformation is obligatory in the case of a string $Wh+X$ which is formed by (6), unless $X = some (one, thing)$...

With this improvement, we come much closer to descriptive adequacy. Still, the question remains whether it is possible to find a principled basis for the factually correct description, in this case. The problem of explanatory adequacy, once again, is that of formulating a general condition on the structure of a transformational grammar that will account for the peculiarities just noted. A plausible solution to this problem is suggested by the observation that relatives and interrogatives differ in another respect as well; namely, in the case of Relativization, the element that is deleted in the embedded (constituent) string still appears in the matrix string, whereas in the case of interrogatives, the deleted element is not represented elsewhere in the sentence. The abstract forms (that is, the categorized terminal strings) underlying a sentence with a relative clause are therefore determinable, given the sentence. This would not be true of interrogatives if a restriction such as that of the preceding paragraph were not imposed. This observation suggests the following general condition on transformational grammar. Each major category has associated with it a "designated element" as a member. This designated element may actually be realized (e.g., *it* for abstract Nouns, *some* (*one, thing*)), or it may be an abstract "dummy element". It is this designated representative of the category that must appear in the underlying strings for those transformations that do not preserve, in the transform, a specification of the actual terminal representative of the category in question. In other words, a transformation can delete an element only if this element is the designated representative of a category, or if the structural condition that defines this transformation states that the deleted element is structurally identical to another element of the transformed string. A deleted element is, therefore, always recoverable.[9]

In conformity with this condition, the rules for forming Noun Phrase-deleting interrogatives (but not relatives or nondeleting interrogatives) must be limited in application to underlying strings containing $Wh + \Sigma$, where Σ is one of these designated elements. It is plausible, on other grounds, that the elements *some* (*one, thing*) are to be identified as designated representatives of the nominal categories. It follows, then, that Noun Phrase-deleting interrogatives must reflect the distributional peculiarities of these designated elements. Hence the general condition on deletion operations just proposed can provide a partial explanation for the peculiar restrictions on the formation of interrogatives in English.

There are indications of a different sort that this condition is necessary for descriptive adequacy. In general, a sentence from

---

[9]   This condition is, incidentally, particularly important for the study of the limits on generative capacity of transformational grammars. It has, in fact, been proposed for reasons totally unrelated to those we are now considering. Cf. Matthews (1961).

which a phrase has been deleted by a grammatical operation is not interpreted as structurally ambiguous. Thus the sentences "his car was stolen" (with agent deletion), "John is eating" (with deletion of Object – for discussion of this class of verbs see Lees, 1960a; Chomsky, 1962a), and so on, are surely not to be considered in the same light as "flying planes can be dangerous", "John doesn't know how good meat tastes," and other familiar examples of structural ambiguity. An elliptical sentence is not simply one that is subject to alternative interpretations. But if it is true that the interpretation of a sentence is determined by the structural descriptions of the strings that underlie it (as is supposed in the theory of transformational grammar), then the degree of ambiguity of a sentence should correlate with the number of different systems of structural description underlying it. In particular, if the condition that we have proposed is not met, the "elliptical sentences" given above should be multiply, in fact, infinitely ambiguous, since they should each have infinitely many sources. Thus "the car was stolen" could derive from "the car was stolen by the boy", "... by the tall boy," "... by the tallest of all the boys in the school", etc. In fact, the proposed condition establishes that each such sentence (similarly, "who did he see?", etc.) is derived from a single source with an unspecified Noun Phrase instead of from infinitely many sources with different Noun Phrases, consistently with the manner in which these sentences are interpreted.

In this case, then, it seems that we can formulate a well-motivated general condition that partially explains the facts stated in the descriptively adequate grammar. This condition predicts that such must be the linguistic intuition of anyone who constructs for himself a transformational grammar to deal with the linguistic data to which he has been exposed.

Further investigation of conditions on relatives and interrogatives raises interesting problems of a variety of different sorts. We have proposed that interrogatives are formed by rule (6), with X limited to Noun Phrases of the form *some* (*one, thing*) *W*. Thus from "I know someone who was expelled" (with W = "who was expelled"), we should derive "who who was expelled do you know?";

from "he has something of yours" (with W = "of yours"), we should derive "what of yours does he have?"; from "I know someone from Philadelphia" (with W = "from Philadelphia"), we should derive "who from Philadelphia do you know?"; and so on. In these cases there are preferred alternatives, namely, "who do you know who was expelled?", "what does he have of yours?", "who do you know from Philadelphia?." Considering these alternatives, we must either modify the rule (6) to allow it to apply only to the segment Determiner + Noun of a Noun Phrase of the form Determiner + Noun + Relative Clause, or we must conclude that the grammar contains a subsidiary rule (7), which applies after (6):

(7) X – relative – Y ⇒ X – Y- relative,

where X is an indefinite Noun Phrase (note that "from Philadelphia", "of yours", have the derived phrase structure *Relative Clause* in the examples above, as does "who was expelled"). The choice between these alternatives is settled by the fact that rule (7) is necessary anyway, to account for such cases as "a man was here who comes from Philadelphia". It seems, then, that these examples do not make it necessary to modify the account of formation of relatives given above. What remains an interesting question, however, is the determination of the conditions under which (7) is optional, obligatory, or excluded, and the determination of its relation to the rule that deletes *who* (*what*) + *Tense* + *be* from relatives. Similarly, some rather subtle questions arise when we consider the problem of Relativization with (6) when X in (6) itself contains a relative clause.

Notice that although several Noun Phrases in a sentence may have *Wh* attached to them, the operation (6) must be limited to a single application to each underlying terminal string. Thus we can have "who saw what?", "you met the man who saw what?", "you read the book that who saw?", "you saw the book which was next to what?", etc., but not "who what saw?", "you saw the book which which was next to" (as a declarative), and so on, as could arise from multiple applications of this rule. These examples show that (6) cannot apply twice to a given string as a Relativization and cannot apply twice as an Interrogative transformation, but it is equally true that it cannot apply to a given string once as a Relativization and once as an Interrogative transformation. Thus if rule (6) has applied to form a string which is embedded as a relative clause, it cannot reapply to this embedded string, preposing one of its Noun Phrases to the full sentence. Thus we can have the interrogative "he saw the man read the book that was on what?", but not "what did he see the man read the book that was on"; and we can have "he wondered where John put what"?, but not "what did he wonder where John put"; etc. Notice that although we can have such sentences as "who did he know who has something of yours" (from "who who has something (of yours) did he know", by rule (7) – similarly, "what did you see the man read that was on the table"?, and so on), we cannot have "what did he know someone who has (of yours")? Thus we can prepose the first, but not the second of the indefinite Noun Phrases of "he knew someone who has something (of yours)", and this, too, is accounted for by the restriction of (6) to a single application to each terminal string.

Because of this constraint, sentences that appear superficially to be rather similar behave quite differently with respect to formation of questions and relatives. Thus consider the sentences (8):

(8) (i)   Mary saw the boy walk towards the railroad station
    (ii) Mary saw the boy who was walking towards the railroad station
    (iii) Mary saw the boy walking towards the railroad station

Sentences (8i) and (8ii) are unambiguous, but have different syntactic analyses. In the case of (8i), the phrase "walk towards the railroad station" is the Complement of the Verb (cf. Chomsky, 1955, 1962), whereas in (8ii), the phrase "who was walking towards the railroad station" is a relative clause forming a single Noun Phrase with "the boy". But (8iii) is subject to either analysis, and is therefore ambiguous, as is obvious when we consider the corresponding passives: "the boy was seen walking towards the railroad station (by Mary)", "the boy walking towards the railroad station was seen (by Mary)". (Notice that there is a further ambiguity, where "Mary" is taken as the subject of walk, but this is irrelevant to the present discussion). But consider the sentence "the railroad station that Mary saw the boy walking towards (towards which Mary saw the boy walking) is about to be demolished". Although this is formed from the structurally ambiguous sentence (8iii), it is quite unambiguous; its relative clause has only the interpretation that is parallel to (8i). Correspondingly, we find that only (8i), and not (8ii), is subject to Relativization of "railroad station". Exactly the same is true of interrogatives. Thus "what did Mary see the boy walking towards"? can have only the interpretation analogous to (8i), although the sentence that is its source can have either interpretation (more accurately, the categorized terminal string that is its unique source happens to be one of two terminal strings that underlie the ambiguous sentence "Mary saw the boy walking towards something"). This configuration of possible interpretations is again a consequence of the constraint just noted, which permits application of (6) to a Noun Phrase within a Verbal Complement, but not to one within a Relative clause.

Example (8) is perfectly typical. To cite just one further case, the sentence "John kept the car in the garage" is ambiguous ("the car was kept in the garage by John," "the car in the garage was kept by John."), but the ambiguity is resolved, in the manner required by the condition under discussion, in "the garage that John kept the car in was demolished," "what did John keep the car in?," etc.

The constraint that (6) may not reapply to a given string is thus necessary if the grammar is to achieve descriptive adequacy. Once again, to achieve the level of explanatory adequacy, we must find a principled basis, a general condition on the structure of any grammar, that will require that in the case of English the rule (6) must be so constrained. Various suggestions come to mind, but I am unable to formulate a general condition that seems to me entirely satisfying.

Finally, it is clear that the first segment Y of the structural condition of rule (6) must be suitably restricted. Thus we cannot have such interrogatives as "what presumably did Bill see" from "presumably Bill saw something", and so on. This suggests that we restrict Y in (6) to the form NP+.... With this further condition, we also succeed in excluding such nonsentences as "what for me to understand would be difficult"?, although the perfectly correct form "what would it be difficult for me to understand"? is still permitted. Thus this condition would account for a distinction between the occurrences of "for me to understand something" in the contexts "– would be difficult" and "it would be difficult –", so far as applicability of (6) is concerned.[10]

This discussion obviously does not exhaust the topic. For one thing, it by no means specifies the distributional peculiarities of relatives and interrogatives in full detail, and to the extent that this deficiency still remains, important questions of explanatory adequacy cannot even be raised. Furthermore, even where a partial explanatory account can be given, there are open questions that we have not dealt with. Thus in discussing designated members of categories we assumed that the representatives of the nominal categories were "someone, something" and their variants, but the examples we gave to support this could equally well have been used to support the claim that the representatives are "everyone, everything". In fact, in favor of the latter claim one might cite such examples as "whose reputations are at stake"? (suggested by P. Kiparsky), which have no source if "someone", "something" are taken as the unique designated elements. But if there are several alternative designated elements, the comments on "recoverability" must be slightly revised. In general, many aspects of relative and interrogative constructions remain to be accounted for, and it seems that the complex of problems relating to rule (6) should continue to provide a profitable testing ground for explanatory hypotheses concerning the form and applicability of grammatical rules.

[10] Alternatively, one might attempt to account for this distinction by a condition that relies on the fact that in the illegitimate case the Noun Phrase to be preposed is contained within a Noun Phrase, while in the legitimate case, it is not. However, the condition that a Noun Phrase contained within a Noun Phrase is not subject to (6), though quite plausible and suggested by many examples, is apparently somewhat too strong, as we can see from such, to be sure, rather marginal examples as "who would you approve of my seeing?", "what are you uncertain about giving to John?", "what would you be surprised by his reading?", etc. There is certainly much more to be said about this matter.

Consider now one final example from the domain of syntax. Such sentences as

(9) I don't approve of his drinking (cooking. driving, etc).

are ambiguous (... the fact that he drinks, cooks, etc.; the manner in which he drinks, cooks, etc.)[11] An explanation for this is proposed in Chomsky (1955), but it can now be given a much better formulation as well as stronger support by several ingenious observations of Lees (1960a, 64f.) and Klima (personal communication). Among the many ways of converting declarative sentences into NP's in English (cf. Lees, 1960a), we have, in particular, two that can be described informally as follows:

(10) $NP - Aux_1 (Aux_2) VP_1 \Rightarrow NP + Possessive - ing (Aux_2) VP_1$
(11) $NP - Aux - Verb - (NP) \Rightarrow NP + Possessive - nom + Verb - (of + NP)$.

The transformation (10) gives such noun phrases as "his refusing (having refused) to participate", "his rejecting the offer", "his (having been) destroying property", etc.; while (11) gives such examples as "his refusal to participate", "his rejection of the offer", "his destruction of property", etc. But the phrases constructed by (10), (11) must be inserted into other sentences in the NP position by a generalized transformation. And this insertion is carried out differently in the two cases. In the case of (10), the transform as a whole replaces the NP of the sentences into which it is inserted; thus the derived Phrase-marker of "his rejecting the offer surprised me"[12] will indicate simply that "his rejecting the offer" is an NP. In the case of (11), however, the element NP + Possessive replaces the Determiner of an NP of the form Determiner + Noun, while the element nom + VP_1 replaces the Noun of this NP.

[11] In the case of "cooking", there are, in fact, two more interpretations, since "cooking" is a Noun independently of the transformations (10), (11), below, and "cook" is one of those Verbs that undergo the transformation of $NP_1 - V - NP_2$ to $NP_2 - V$ (cf. Gleitman, 1960; Chomsky, 1962a) giving "NP cooks" (which is then subject to (10)) from "Unspecified Noun Phrase cooks NP".
[12] For discussion of how transformations impose derived phrase structure, see Chomsky (1955, 1961a), Matthews (1962), Postal (1962).

LIBRARY ST. MARY'S COLLEGE

Thus the derived Phrase-marker of "his rejection of the offer surprised me" will indicate that "his rejection of the offer" is an NP, that "his" is a Determiner and that "rejection of the offer" is a Noun. There are several facts that motivate this decision. For one thing, note that in the case of the phrases formed by (11) (but not those formed by (10)), adjectives can be inserted. Thus we can have "his strange refusal to participate", "his unexpected rejection of the offer", "his wanton destruction of property", etc.; but not "his strange refusing to participate", "his unexpected rejecting the offer", "his wanton destroying property". But adjectives are introduced by transformation[13] in the position Determiner – Noun. Consequently, for the adjectivalization transformation to operate properly, this structure must be specified in the derived Phrase-marker of the NP formed by (11). Secondly, note that the position of the "NP + Possessive" construction in an NP formed by (11), but not (10), can be filled by "the" ("the refusal to participate", "the rejection of the offer", "the destruction of property"; but not "the refusing to participate", "the rejecting the offer", "the destroying property"). This indicates that paired with (11) is an otherwise identical operation that replaces the Noun of the matrix sentence by "nom + Verb (of NP)", leaving the Determiner "the" unaffected, and again shows that the paired transformation (11) replaces the Determiner (which is, in fact, "the") of the matrix sentence by the "NP + Possessive" construction, which thus takes on the structure Determiner by the general rule for substitution transformations (cf. references of note 12).

But now observe that although (9) is ambiguous, both (12) and (13) are quite unambiguous:

(12) I don't approve of his drinking the beer (driving a sports car)
(13) I don't approve of his excessive drinking (careless driving).

Furthermore, they have opposite interpretations. Thus (12) refers

---

[13] In Chomsky (1955, 1962a) this is given as a separate adjectivalization transformation, but J. Applegate has pointed out that modifying adjectives must rather be introduced by a transformation of sentences with relative clauses, as proposed, in fact, in the Port-Royal grammar - cf. p. 15 above; and this proposal has been adopted in Lees (1960), Smith (1961).

to the fact of his drinking the beer, driving a sports car, etc.; while (13) refers to the manner of his drinking (of the beer), of his driving, etc. The fact that adjectives can appear in (13) implies that in this case the phrases "his drinking", "his driving", etc., have the derived phrase structure Determiner-Noun, as in the case of "his rejection of the offer". They must thus be formed by the transformation (11). And observe, in fact, that there is no other nominalized form of these verbs (as "refusal" and "rejection" contrast with "refusing" and "rejecting"). Hence we conclude that there is an obligatory rule that assigns to the nominalizing morpheme *nom* introduced in (11) the shape /ing/ when it is affixed to "drink", "drive", etc., just as it assigns to *nom* the shape /æl/ when it is affixed to "refuse" and the shape /yin/ when it is affixed to "reject".

It follows that "drinking", "driving", etc., will be formed in two distinct ways, by (10) and by (11). Since these verbs are, furthermore, optionally intransitive, the full NP "his drinking", "his driving", etc., will also be generated in two ways, once by (10) (with the derived structure NP and the interpretation "fact that") and once by (11) (with the derived structure Determiner + Noun, as well as NP, and the interpretation "manner of"). Noting that adjectives cannot be inserted in (12) (giving, e.g., "I don't approve of his excessive drinking the beer"), we conclude that this is unambiguously derived by (9), consistent with its interpretation, in this case.

Notice that as the wh-question transformation was formulated, it does not yield "whose book (did you find)?", "which book (did you find)?", etc. To provide these, it must be extended to apply also to underlying strings of the form X – Determiner + Noun – Y (note that possessive NP's are Determiners, replacing the definite article, in fact, by a transformation). Applying this observation to the present case, we see that this transformation will yield "whose excessive drinking surprised you?" etc., as it should, but that it will exclude "whose drinking the beer surprised you?", etc. (again, correctly), since the underlying NP in this case is not of the form Determiner + Noun. Similarly, "whose drinking surprised you?" will be derived from only one source (and it is, in fact, unambiguous), since only one of the potential sources is of the required form Determiner + Noun.

See Katz and Postal (forthcoming) for further discussion of the problems presented by such examples as (9), and for several new and interesting ideas as to how they should be solved. It seems clear that examples such as these are totally beyond the range of any version of the taxonomic model, as so far conceived. But again, it seems possible to reach the levels of descriptive and even explanatory adequacy with a transformational grammar.

2.3. LEVELS OF ADEQUACY IN SEMANTICS

I have given several examples of how a higher level of adequacy might be achieved by linguistic theory in the domains of phonology and syntax. It remains to consider the third major part of a synchronic description, namely, its semantic aspect. Here the problem is much more obscure. One might perhaps maintain that the condition of observational adequacy would be met by an account of situational regularities associated with actual discourse;[14] and that the condition of descriptive adequacy is achieved by a set of appropriately interrelated dictionary entries and "projection rules" (in the sense of Katz and Fodor, 1963), an explicit portrayal of the structure of certain "semantic fields", an account of terms that enter into specific meaning-relations, e.g., synonymy, etc.

How might one hope to achieve a higher level of adequacy, in this case? It might plausibly be maintained that certain semantic features of a language can be partially explained in terms of underlying syntactic processes. As an example, consider the discussion of (9), above. Or consider the case of such adjectives as "interesting", "astonishing", "intriguing", etc., which have the semantic property that they are "connected with a specific human 'reaction',"[15] even where no explicit reference is made to the person

[14] What are called "semantical regularities" by Ziff (1960a).
[15] Cf. Nowell-Smith (1954, 85). Other adjectives may also be characterizable in this way for some different reason, but this is irrelevant to the correctness of the present observation.

who is interested, astonished, intrigued ("it was an intriguing plan", as distinct from "it was an elaborate plan", etc.). These adjectives have in common many important syntactic features that distinguish them from other Verb + ing forms (e.g., "the plan seems intriguing (*failing)", "a very intriguing (*failing) plan", etc.). Furthermore, they would be derived, in a transformational grammar, from sentences in which they appear as Verbs ("the plan intrigues one", etc. – cf. Chomsky, 1962a). But the class of verbs from which these adjectives derive are pure transitives with human objects.[16] Thus the structural description of the sentence "it was an intriguing plan", as provided by a transformational grammar, will contain the terminal string underlying "the plan intrigued one (i.e., unspecified human)" just as explicitly as it contains the past tense morpheme; and this fact might be suggested as the explanation for the cited semantic feature.

In general, as syntactic description becomes deeper, what appear to be semantic questions fall increasingly within its scope;[17] and it is not entirely obvious whether or where one can draw a natural bound between grammar and "logical grammar", in the sense of Wittgenstein and the Oxford philosophers. Nevertheless, it seems clear that explanatory adequacy for descriptive semantics requires, beyond this, the development of an independent semantic theory (analogous, perhaps, to the theory of universal phonetics as discussed briefly below) that deals with questions of a kind that can scarcely be coherently formulated today, in particular, with the question: what are the substantive and formal constraints on systems of con-

---

[16] That is, "intrigue", "astonish", etc. do not undergo optional deletion of the object, as do "cook", "eat", etc.; and such sentences as "John amused the book" are clearly deviant. These observations are not refuted by the fact that deviant utterances with object deletion can be attested (cf., e.g., Edmund Wilson, *The American Earthquake*, Doubleday, 1958, 481: "The American Legion Posts, which dominate the later sections, startle, trouble and shock", where all three verbs belong to the category in question), just as the distinction between the classes of adjectives noted above is not obscured by instances such as "if the sea was not *very* raging, ..." (Bertrand Russell, *Inquiry into Meaning and Truth*, W. W. Norton & Co., 1940, 84). See note 2 of § 1 and references there.

[17] For discussion see Harris (1954), Chomsky (1957a), Ziff (1960a), Katz and Fodor (1963), Katz and Postal (forthcoming).

cepts that are constructed by humans on the basis of presented data? Observe that the problem posed in § 1 for general linguistics is a special case of this question, where the system of concepts that is acquired consists of the notions "well-formed sentence of L", "grammatical relation in L", "sound pattern of L", etc. Perhaps it is not too much to hope that this particular problem may serve as a useful paradigm case. We return to this speculation below in § 5. In any event, it seems that formulation of a general semantic theory of some sort, independent of any particular lanuage, is perhaps not an unreasonable task to undertake, and is a precondition for any far-reaching attempt to attain a level of explanatory adequacy in semantic description.

We might observe, at this point, that many problems of universal semantics (as of universal phonetics) were raised and quite seriously studied in the seventeenth century (cf., for example, Wilkins, 1668), though rarely since.

2.4. COMPREHENSIVENESS OF GRAMMARS

In the preceding discussion, three levels of adequacy have been loosely sketched that might be attained by a linguistic description in the areas of phonology, syntax, and semantics. Of these, only the levels of descriptive and explanatory adequacy (and, ultimately, only the latter) are of sufficient interest to justify further discussion. Notice, however, that these levels of success are discussed only for grammars that are paired with some linguistic theory. It is always possible to describe the linguistic intuition of the native speaker in a completely ad hoc way in any particular case if we drop the requirement that the grammar be constructed in accordance with some fixed model or if we allow the associated linguistic theory to be completely general and without content (e.g., if our linguistic theory merely states that a grammar is an arbitrary computer program). Presumably, this possibility needs no further discussion. It is important to bear in mind that a grammar that assigns correctly the mass of structural descriptions (remote as this is from present hopes) would still be of no particular linguistic interest unless it also were to provide some insight into those formal properties that distinguish a natural language from arbitrary, enumerable sets of structural descriptions. At best, such a grammar would help to clarify the subject matter for linguistic theory, just as a fourteenth century clock depicting the positions of the heavenly bodies merely posed, but did not even suggest an answer to the questions to which classical physics addressed itself.

In connection with the question of levels of success, we must also briefly consider the matter of coverage of data. Sapir's often quoted remark that "all grammars leak" is extremely misleading, insofar as it implies that there are grammars so comprehensive that the question of completeness of coverage can seriously be raised. But this is patently false. In the case of traditional (i.e., inexplicit generative) grammars, the gaps are not easy to locate because of the vagueness of the rules and the essential reliance on the linguistic intuition of the reader. One of the merits of an explicit generative grammar is that these gaps are immediately exposed. Anyone who is actively at work on a linguistic description can cite innumerable examples that fall beyond the range of rules as so far formulated, or that are incorrectly handled by these rules – it is, in fact, sufficient to open a book or to listen to a conversation at random to find countless examples of sentences and sentence types that are not adequately dealt with in traditional or modern grammars.

Comprehensiveness of coverage does not seem to me to be a serious or significant goal in the present stage of linguistic science. Gross coverage of data can be achieved in many ways, by grammars of very different forms. Consequently, we learn little about the nature of linguistic structure from the study of grammars that merely accomplish this. Higher levels of adequacy, in the sense described above, have been achieved so far only in limited areas. But it is only by studying the properties of grammars that achieve higher levels of adequacy and by gradually increasing the scope of description without sacrificing depth of analysis that we can hope to sharpen and extend our understanding of the nature of linguistic structure.

It is important to bear this in mind in considering the masses of linguistic data that lie beyond the scope of an explicit generative grammar, proposed for some fragment of a language. It is no criticism of such a grammar to point to data that is not encompassed by its rules, where this data has no demonstrated bearing on the correctness of alternative formulations of the grammar of this language or on alternative theories of language. Until incorporated in an explicit generative grammar, such examples simply stand as exceptions, no more relevant to the correctness of the already formulated rules than strong verbs and irregular plurals. Listing of innumerable examples is neither difficult nor very interesting; it is quite another matter to find rules that account for them, or a general theory of such rules.[18]

It is necessary to distinguish between exceptions to a grammar, and counter-examples to a proposed general theory of linguistic structure. Examples that lie beyond the scope of a grammar are quite innocuous unless they show the superiority of some alternative grammar. They do not show that the grammar as already

---

[18]   These comments apply, it seems to me, to most of the examples presented by Bolinger (1960, 1961). These lists of examples could be extended indefinitely. In the form in which they are presented, they have, for the most part, no obvious bearing on the correctness of formulations of English grammar that have been proposed for certain fragments of the language, or of the theories that underlie them.

Bolinger does suggest (1961, 381) that his examples are in conflict with certain theories of generative grammar, and that they support an alternative view about the nature of language, about which he offers only the following hint: in a grammar of the sort he envisions, "constructions are not produced one from another or from a stock of abstract components, but filed side by side", and the speakers do not 'produce' constructions, but rather "'reach for' them, from a preestablished inventory". It is difficult to comment on the proposal in this form, because of the vagueness of the notions "construction" and "filed". If by "construction" Bolinger means something like "sequence of word classes", then his proposal is ruled out at once. It is clear that the variety of normal sentences is so great that the number of word class sequences associated with them is far larger than the number of seconds in a lifetime. For quantitative estimates bearing on this question (which are furthermore highly conservative) see Miller, Galanter, Pribram (1960), Miller and Chomsky (1963). If he has in mind some more abstract principle by which constructions are "filed", it remains to be seen whether this proposal, when clearly formulated, will differ from current theories of generative grammar.

formulated is incorrect. Examples that contradict the principles formulated in some general theory show that, to at least this extent, the theory is incorrect and needs revision. Such examples become important if they can be shown to have some bearing on alternative conceptions of linguistic structure.

3

ON OBJECTIVITY OF LINGUISTIC DATA

When we discuss the levels of descriptive and explanatory adequacy, questions immediately arise concerning the firmness of the data in terms of which success is to be judged (nor are difficulties lacking even on the level of observational adequacy – cf. note 1, § 2) For example, in the case of (3), (4) of p. 34 one might ask how we can establish that the two are sentences of different types, or that "John's eagerness to please..." is well-formed, while "John's easiness to please..." is not, and so on. There is no very satisfying answer to this question; data of this sort are simply what constitute the subject matter for linguistic theory. We neglect such data at the cost of destroying the subject. It is not that these introspective judgments are sacrosanct and beyond any conceivable doubt. On the contrary, their correctness can be challenged and supported in many ways, some quite indirect. Consistency among speakers of similar backgrounds, as well as for a particular speaker on different occasions, is relevant information. The possibility of constructing a systematic and general theory to account for these observations is also a factor to be considered in evaluating the probable correctness of particular observations (as in the case of any data – cf. note 1, § 2). Consequently the fact that a certain grammatical theory has had explanatory value in dealing with data from one language may be an important factor in determining the validity of data from some different language. Operational tests that consistently supported introspective judgment in clear cases would, were they available, also be relevant in determining the correctness of particular observations.

It is sometimes assumed that operational criteria have a special and privileged position, in this connection, but this is surely a mistake. For one thing, we can be fairly certain that there will be no operational criteria for any but the most elementary notions.

Furthermore, operational tests, just as explanatory theories, must meet the condition of correspondence to introspective judgment, if they are to be at all to the point. Thus a test of degree of grammaticalness that failed to make a distinction between, e.g., "colorless green ideas sleep furiously" and "furiously sleep ideas green colorless" would, to this extent, prove itself to be an uninteresting test. When a criterion (operational or not) is proposed for some notion, we must first inquire whether the concept it delimits is at all close to the one in which we are interested.

It is surprising how frequently this point is overlooked. Thus many linguists have proposed that synonymy be measured somehow in terms of degree of distributional similarity (cf., e.g., Hoenigswald, 1960; Frei, 1961), and have then concluded that such pairs as "bachelor" and "unmarried man" are not synonymous, since one, but not the other, can occur in the context – hood, etc. But all that this observation shows is that the proposed criterion is entirely wrong, as, indeed, it clearly is.[1] However synonymy may ultimately be analyzed, it is a fact that a speaker of English need undertake no empirical investigation to determine whether some bachelors are married, as he must to determine whether some bachelors are redhaired; and such facts as this provide the basis for the conclusion that there is a meaning relation between "bachelor" and "unmarried man". A proposed characterization (such as the proposed distributional analysis) of these

[1] A critical and still unanswered objection to any such approach has been given by Bar-Hillel (1954, 233). Frei also gives a "distributional" argument against the existence of homonyms (40), but again this is simply a proposal for terminological revision. He regards these terminological innovations as refuting the position (argued in Chomsky, 1957a) that there is no evidence for the claim that the notion of phonemic contrast can be defined in terms of sameness of meaning in a way which will provide a semantic basis for phonology. But in fact, he mistakes the question at issue, which was this: given a set of sentence tokens to which meaning is somehow assigned, can this information be used to determine which of these tokens contrast? Presumably, those who maintain that phonology can or must be based on meaning are claiming that the answer is affirmative. But if Frei is correct in assuming (41-2) that meaning can be assigned only to an element of *langue*, not to tokens (as, in fact, is also argued in Chomsky, 1957a, 98), then the claim under discussion is automatically shown to be vacuous.

meaning relations which is inconsistent with these facts is, to that extent, shown to be wrong or irrelevant.

Similarly, consider Quine's proposed quasi-operational definition of a concept of "stimulus meaning" (1960). As this is defined, the stimulus meaning of a word varies widely with level of attention, set, gullibility, mood, visual acuity, cortical lesions, etc., while the meaning and reference of a term are independent of these factors. These, and the many further discrepancies[2] suggest that the concept has little relevance to the study of meaning and reference; consequently, it is not at all clear why any serious consideration should be given to this particular operational test. Quine's concern with it appears to stem from his belief that it provides all of the objective information that can be obtained about any language (e.g., 39), and that all additional assumptions about a language are "arbitrary" and "unverifiable" (71–2, 90) since they are "undetermined by the speech dispositions" and might conceivably be "due to linguistic ingenuity or lucky coincidence" (Quine's thesis of "indeterminacy of translation", and, also, of grammar, since he regards grammar as somehow based on translation – cf. 68f.). But he offers no argument for the belief that this particular operational test, among the many that might be proposed, has some unique significance; and the thesis of indeterminacy seems to amount only to the assertion that a significant empirical assertion has logically conceivable alternatives, which is true but unexciting.[3]

[2] The stimulation X belongs to the (affirmative) stimulus meaning of the sentence Y if presentation of X prompts assent to Y (with various qualifications that are not relevant here). But in general, an object is correctly called a Y not just because of its appearance, but because of its function, or even its "history" (cf. comments by P. Foot, 1961, 47f; in fact, the general point is clear and explicit in Aristotle). The other notions defined in terms of "stimulus meaning" are likewise of dubious interest. Thus "stimulus analyticity", as defined, would seem to hold of many universally shared beliefs (e.g., "there have been some black dogs" - cf. Quine, 1960, p. 66- or "the world is flat", at one period), and thus sheds little light on the important (but, as Quine has elsewhere demonstrated, quite obscure) notion of "connection of meaning".

[3] What seems open to question in this account is only the use of the words "arbitrary" and "unverifiable" to apply to empirical hypotheses that do not "merely summarize evidence, that is, to all non-trivial assertions of science or common sense, to X's belief that Y is using "tomorrow" in the sense of X's

In these and many other cases, what has not been shown is that the concept defined by the proposed operational criterion has some importance. In fact, at the present stage of the study of language, it seems rather obvious that the attempt to gain some insight into the range of data that we now have is likely to be far more fruitful than the attempt to make this data more firm, e.g., by tests for synonymy, grammaticalness, and the like. Operational criteria for these notions, were they available and correct, might soothe the scientific conscience; but how in fact, would they advance our understanding of the nature of language, or of the use and acquisition of language?

"tomorrow" and not his "yesterday", etc. Furthermore, it seems that Quine's own discussions of indeterminacy of reference (e.g., 52f.; cf. also 78–9) should be unintelligible, on his own grounds, for his hypothesis that his readers do not understand his "rabbit" in the sense of "rabbit stage", etc., is "unverifiable" and "arbitrary", as he uses these terms.

Notice, in this connection, that though given a finite amount of evidence, it is trivially true that there are conflicting hypotheses compatible with it, it does not follow that there are certain conflicting hypotheses among which no decision can be made by any possible obtainable evidence. Given a decision to restrict evidence to "stimulus meaning", one no doubt could find irresolvable conflicts, but this would be an uninteresting consequence of an arbitrary decision.

4

THE NATURE OF STRUCTURAL DESCRIPTIONS

4.0. A generative grammar consists of a *syntactic component*, which generates strings of formatives and specifies their structural features and interrelations; a *phonological component*, which converts a string of formatives with a specified (surface) syntactic structure into a phonetic representation; and a *semantic component*, which assigns a semantic interpretation to a string of formatives with a specified (deep) syntactic structure. After a brief discussion of structural descriptions on the syntactic level, we will turn to a more detailed account of alternative views as to the nature of phonological representation. For discussion of semantic interpretation of structures generated by the syntactic component, see Katz and Fodor (1963), Katz and Postal (forthcoming).

4.1. THE SYNTACTIC COMPONENT

A structural description on the syntactic level must indicate how a string of formatives is subdivided into constituents of varying scope (from formatives, at one extreme, to the full sentence, at the other) and what are the categories to which these substrings belong (Noun, Verb, Noun Phrase, Relative clause, etc.).[1] Such information can be presented as a labelled bracketing of a string of formatives or in some equivalent notation, e.g., a labelled tree such as (14) for the sentences (3), (4), of § 2.2.

[1] The goal of traditional "universal grammar" was, of course, to give a substantive general account of these categories, thus fixing a universal "vocabulary" for the (generative) grammars of all languages. Presumably, such fixed universal category symbols would have to be defined in terms of formal properties of grammars and, perhaps, language-independent semantic properties of some sort. Whatever the feasibility of this enterprise may be, we will not consider it here, and will regard the category names for the time being as only conventional.

(14)

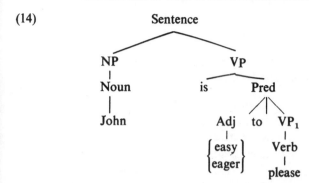

Such a representation is what we have called a *Phrase-marker*. In terms of such Phrase-markers, we can define grammatical relations, as certain subconfigurations. Thus the Subject-Predicate relation might be identified as the subconfiguration (Sentence; NP, VP), in which case it would hold between "John" and "is easy (eager) to please" in (14); and the Verb-Object relation could be defined as the configuration (VP$_1$; Verb, NP), in which case it would hold between "please" and "John" in "this may please John", with the obvious Phrase-marker; etc. Alternatively, these relations can be defined in terms of the heads of such configurations. For detailed proposals along these lines, see Chomsky (1955, chapter 6). It is the great merit of Pike's recent work in tagmemics to have focussed attention on the importance of these traditional notions, although the tagmemic method of analysis of these relational notions is both redundant and (since it is a strictly categorial interpretation) not adequate – see Postal (1964, section VII).

Whatever exact decisions are made, it is evident, as observed in § 2, above, that a great deal of relevant information is not representable in terms of a single Phrase-marker such as (14). Thus there is no way to indicate, in such a representation, that when the adjective is "easy", the relation of "please" to "John" in (14) is that of Verb-Object, as in "this pleases John"; and that when the adjective is "eager" and is not followed by "for + NP", the relation of "John" to "please" in (14) is that of Subject-Verb, as in "John pleases us". Similarly, there is no way to indicate by a single labelled bracketing that in the sentence (15) the expressions "John", "please" and "gift" are related as they are in (16):

(15) did John expect to be pleased by the gift?

(16) The gift pleased John.

For reasons such as this, the taxonomic model of modern linguistics (cf. § 1, above), which provides a single Phrase-marker of the type of (14) as the structural description of a string, must be regarded as descriptively inadequate.

One might attempt to overcome this inadequacy by extending the definition of "grammatical relation" in the following way. Let us say that a grammatical relation holds of a certain pair (triple, etc.) of expressions (I) if they form part of a configuration of a Phrase-marker, as described above, or (II) if a "co-occurrence relation" of an appropriate sort[2] holds between the pair in question and a

---

[2] For a careful definition of one such notion, see Hiż (1961). This notion was introduced by Harris (1952a, 1952b) and studied in detail (Harris, 1957) as the basis for a theory of grammatical transformations. It is also mentioned in a similar connection by Bazell (1953), and is applied to Russian by Worth (1958). A grammatical transformation is defined, from this point of view, as a (symmetrical) relation holding between two sentence forms if corresponding positions in the two forms are filled by the same n-tuples of expressions. This relation is not part of generative grammar, as is the notion "grammatical transformation" of § 1 and the references cited there, but is a structural relation holding of sentences and sentence forms generated by a taxonomic, IC grammar (as in Harris, 1951a, chapter 16). The notions of "co-occurrence relation" and "generative transformation" are rather different in formal properties as well as in their role in actual syntactic description, and a great deal of confusion can result from failure to distinguish them. Thus it makes no sense to arrange co-occurrence relations "in sequence", but generative transformations can (and, in practice, must) be ordered and applied in sequence. The examples of § 2 depend essentially on appropriate ordering and sequential application of transformational rules, and on appropriate choice of base versus derived forms (a distinction which is also not definable in terms of co-occurrence). Furthermore, co-occurrence is a relation defined on actual sentences, while generative transformations apply to abstract structures that often bear no close relation to actual sentences. Note also that in a generative transformational grammar, a direct, one-step transformational relation would hold between (16) and each of the sentences of (17); a somewhat more devious relation would hold between (16) and (15), which is derived by a sequence of transformations from a pair of strings, one of which underlies (16); and no relation at all would hold between (15)-(17i), or (17i)-(17ii), though all would be based on the terminal string under-

pair that has this grammatical relation in the sense of (I). Accordingly, we would say that in

(17) (i) did the gift please John?
      (ii) John was pleased by the gift.

where the grammatical relations are not expressible directly in terms of subconfigurations of the Phrase-marker, the Subject-Verb and Verb-Object relations hold of the pairs "the gift" – "please" and "please" – "John", respectively, because any triple of expressions that can replace "the gift", "please" and "John" in (17) can also (with appropriate reordering) fill the positions of these expressions in (16), where the grammatical relations are definable directly in terms of the Phrase-marker.

However, this approach seems to me to face insurmountable objections. Thus although it is true that a co-occurrence relation of the appropriate sort may hold between (16) and (17), it does not hold between (15) and (16), or (18i) and (16). Thus "please" – "John" can be replaced by "bring" – "happiness" in (16), but not in (15) or in (18i); but in all three cases these expressions are related as Verb-Object. And if some modification is proposed to deal with this discrepancy, will it be able to distinguish the grammatically related "please" – "John" in (15) from the same pair, grammatically unrelated, in "did John expect you to be pleased by the gift?" Or consider the sentences (18ii-iv):

lying (16). From the point of view of co-occurrence, however, there is a "one-step" relation between both (16)-(17), and (17i)-(17ii), and no relation at all (because of "the gift brought happiness", etc.) between (15) and (16). Similarly, no co-occurrence relation would hold between (18iii) and (18ii) (because of "I met the boy"), though the latter is derived from the former by a sequence of generative transformations. There are many other differences. In connection with these remarks, recall the qualifications of note 8, p. 38, above.

Harris' notion of transformation as a co-occurrence relation developed in the course of his work in the late 1940's on analysis of the structure of extended discourse. At the time, I was attempting to construct generative grammars for Modern Hebrew and English using Harris' morpheme-to-utterance procedures, with variables ranging over "long components", as a model for the syntactic component. There were serious difficulties in this, and the notion of grammatical transformation, when adapted and redesigned to enter the syntactic component of a generative grammar with ordered rules, seemed to overcome most of these.

(18) (i)   the gift pleased John but not Bill
     (ii) the book is what I want
     (iii) I want the book
     (iv) the clever boy saw the friendly man

In both (18ii) and (18iii), the Verb-Object relation holds of the pair "want" – "the book"; but only in (18iii) can this pair be replaced by "met" – "the boy". In (18iv), "clever" and "boy" are related as in "the boy is clever"; but in the latter, though not in (18iv), the pair "plan" – "intriguing" can replace "boy" – "clever". Furthermore, it seems that any pair that can replace "clever" – "boy" in (18iv) can replace "clever" – "man" in the same sentence, though no grammatical relation at all holds of this pair.

It is, of course, impossible to show that no possible modification of the notion of co-occurrence could deal with such problems. However, for the present it seems clear that any theory which, like the theory of phrase structure grammar, assigns a single Phrase-marker such as (14) to an utterance, is incapable of expressing deeper structural relations and must therefore be ruled out by considerations of descriptive adequacy.[3]

In the case of a transformational grammar, the syntactic description of a string of formatives consists of a set of *underlying Phrase-markers* (one for each of the underlying simple strings from which the string is derived), a *derived Phrase-marker* such as (14) that gives its surface constituent structure, and a *Transformation-marker* that expresses the manner of its derivation from underlying strings.[4] The deeper structural information in the examples that we have discussed is provided by the underlying Phrase-markers (for further details concerning the particular example (14), see Miller and Chomsky, 1963; see the references cited previously for the other cases). These examples are quite typical in this respect. In general, the grammatical relations that are expressed (in the manner

---

[3] Many other difficulties in the theory of phrase structure grammar are discussed in Chomsky (1955, 1957a, 1961a). Postal, 1961, 1964.
[4] For discussion of these matters, see the references of note 12, on page 47. There are many open and difficult questions here, but the general outlines of a satisfactory theory seem clear.

indicated above) in the underlying Phrase-markers are those that constitute the deeper structure and that determine the semantic interpretation of an utterance. The categorization expressed in the derived Phrase-marker plays a role in determining the form of the utterance (thus the "grammatical Subject" determines the number of the Verb Phrase, and the derived Phrase-marker determines the functioning of the phonological rules – cf. the references of note 6, p. 14) but is irrelevant to its content. The primary motivation for the theory of transformational grammar lies in the fact that the significant grammatical functions and relations are expressed, in a natural way, only in underlying elementary Phrase-markers. For the present, the transformational model for generative grammar is unique in that it allows for the generation of structural information of a variety rich enough to account for facts of the kind discussed here and in § 2, above – and, furthermore, to do so in many cases in a principled way, thus reaching the higher level of explanatory adequacy – though it is by no means without its problems.

4.2. THE PHONOLOGICAL COMPONENT

The phonological component of the grammar can be regarded as an input-output device which operates on a string of formatives, provided with a structural analysis by the syntactic component, and assigns to this string a representation as a string of phones. It is, in part, an open question to what extent structural information on the syntactic level is relevant to determining the phonetic form of a string of formatives. There is no doubt that information of the kind provided in the derived Phrase-marker is essential,[5] and there are scattered examples that suggest that deeper syntactic features may also play a role in determining the details of phonetic shape.

A rather classical view of the structure of the phonological component might be something like this. Formatives are of two types: grammatical and lexical (among the grammatical we count,

[5] See the references of note 6, § 1, and notes 4 and 5 of § 2 for details. All of these studies are based on the notion "transformational cycle" sketched in § 1.

as subtypes, class markers and junctural elements introduced by syntactic rules, e.g., word boundary). Each grammatical formative is represented by a single symbol. Each lexical formative is represented in a systematic orthography as a string of symbols, each of which is assigned to certain categories (Vowel, Consonant, Voiced, etc.). Each symbol can, in fact, be regarded as an abbreviation for the set of categories to which it belongs, and each lexical item can thus be represented by a *classificatory matrix* in which the columns stand for what we may call "segments" and the rows, for categories; the entry in the ith row and j^{th} column indicates whether the jth segment belongs to the ith category. These categories we may call (classificatory) distinctive features. Some squares of the matrix may be blank, where the feature in question can be supplied by a general rule (e.g., the entry for Rounding in the case of English Lax Front Vowels, which become, automatically, unrounded).

The rules of the phonological component are ordered, and apply in sequence to the string of formatives (utilizing, when this is relevant, the associated syntactic information) until ultimately a representation in terms of a universal phonetic alphabet is reached. The symbols of this alphabet are specified in terms of a set of phonetic features; hence the output of the phonological component can again be regarded as a matrix in which columns represent phones and rows, phonetic features of the universal system. The entry in the ith row and j^{th} column indicates whether the jth phone of the generated utterance possesses the ith feature, or the degree to which it possesses this feature (in the case of such features as stress). Classificatory distinctive features are by definition "binary"; phonetic features may or may not be. A representation in terms of phonetic features we may call a *phonetic matrix*, again regarding the symbols of the universal phonetic alphabet as mere conventional abbreviations for sets of feature specifications.

The universal phonetic alphabet is part of a universal phonetic theory. In addition to a fixed set of features, such a theory should contain general laws concerning possible combinations and contrasts. Steps toward such a theory are found in the work of the classical British phoneticians (Bell, Ellis, Sweet); in the "phonologie" of de Saussure's 1897 lectures[6] and again in Jakobson's theory of distinctive features and phonetic universals (e.g., Jakobson, Fant and Halle, 1952). This theory constitutes a part of general linguistic theory, exactly as do the restrictions on the form of rules and the other constraints on the structure of a generative grammar. We will refer to the requirement that a general linguistic theory must incorporate a universal phonetic theory, with a fixed alphabet, as the condition of *phonetic specifiability*. Note that a universal phonetic alphabet is the counterpart of a substantive theory of syntactic categories (see note 1, § 4) that assigns a fixed significance to the labels used in the syntactic component; but in the case of a phonetic alphabet, the construction of a concrete and substantive theory has, of course, been much more fully realized.

[6] Thus, for example, he claims that Nasalization is never distinctive for liquids in any language (1916, 74), and consequently need not be specified in the representation of, e.g., the nasalized /l/ of French "branlant". If this is true, then Nasalization need not be specified for liquids in the phonetic matrix for any language, just as Rounding need not be specified for Lax Front Vowels in the classificatory matrices of English. It is worth noting that there are much earlier studies of articulatory phonetics with a view towards establishing a universal phonetic theory, for example, in the English grammatical tradition, the extensive distinctive features analysis developed by Wallis, Wilkins and others in the seventeenth century. It is difficult to imagine what might be the basis for the fairly commonly held view that Western scholars, prior to the nineteenth century, "had not observed the sounds of speech, and confused them with the written symbols of the alphabet" (Bloomfield, 1933, p. 8). In fact, Aristotle observes that "spoken words are the symbols of mental experience and written words are the symbols of spoken words" (*De Interpretatione*), and the truism that writing is a derivative system is repeated frequently in grammatical studies. Furthermore, there was serious investigation of articulatory phonetics, as noted above, well before the nineteenth century. In the same connection, it is worth mentioning that the widely held view (cf. again Bloomfield, 1933, chapter 1) that early modern "general grammar" was typically prescriptive and wedded to a Latin model (or a "logical model") is also quite false. Thus, for example, the *Grammaire générale et raisonnée* (often taken as the prototype of this tendency) suggests interesting analyses of the syntax of French, and (so far as "prescriptiveness" is concerned) establishes the following maxim (82–3) which "ceux qui travaillent sur une langue vivante, doivent toujours avoir devant les yeux," namely, "que les façons de parler qui sont autorisées par un usage général et non-contesté, doivent passer pour bonnes, encore qu'elles soient contraires aux règles et à l'analogie de la langue" (though it goes on, quite correctly, to warn against the absurdity of misuse or misevaluation of such "bizarreries de l'usage.").

Let us assume that at a certain stage in the application of the rules of the phonological component, all grammatical formatives except junctures will have been eliminated and we have a representation in terms of classificatory matrices and junctures alone (with derived phrase structure indicated). At this point, for example, English "saw", which at the input stage is /sī/ + *past*, might be represented /sɔ/ (though English "heard", which at the input stage might be /hīr/ + past, might be represented /hīr≠d/, since the general rules the convert ī to e in many contexts, and that convert lax, non-compact vowels to [ɨ] before final /r/ (+ Consonant), would presumably not yet have applied). Similarly, at this stage, such a phrase as "telegraphic code" (at the phonetic level, perhaps [tʰelɨgræfikkʰɔwd]) would still be represented /tele + græf + ik # kōd/, or, more fully,

(19) [NP[Adj[N[Pre tele] [Stem græf]] ik] # [N kōd]],

where the notation [A x], with paired brackets, indicates that the bracketed string x is a string of the category A. This representation in terms of segments and junctures, with the derived constituent structure of the string still marked (since it plays a role in the determination of phonetic shape by subsequent phonological rules), we will call, tentatively, the level of *systematic phonemics*, implying by the word "systematic" that the choice of elements at this level is deeply determined by properties of both the syntactic and the phonological component. The representation in terms of phones (and, possibly, phonetic junctures) that constitutes the output of the phonological component, we will call the level of *systematic phonetics*.

So far as I can see, there is no other significant level of representation that can be isolated in the phonological component. The input to the phonological component is, in effect, the lowest level of syntactic representation ("l'étage inférieur de la morphologie" of de Saussure, cf. Godel, 1957, 166) where segments are classified in terms of what will ultimately be phonetic characteristics ("caractères phoniques", *op. cit.*). The output of this component, as mentioned above, is essentially de Saussure's "phonologie", or the "narrow transcription" of the British phoneticians. The level of systematic phonemics is, essentially, the "phonological orthography" of Sapir (cf. Sapir, 1933), his "ideal sounds" and "true elements of the phonetic pattern" (cf. 1925, note 2); whereas systematic phonetics is his "phonetic orthography" (1933) or "objective phonemes" (1925). Similarly, systematic phonemics seems to be, in essence, the phonemics of Bloomfield's practice (1933) (in particular, when his "secondary phonemes" are not represented), though it is difficult to say whether it is in accord with his phonological theory, which is hardly a model of clarity.[7] Systematic phonemics would now generally be called "morphophonemics", in one of the several senses of this term. This terminological innovation is justified if there is a third, intermediate level of systematic representation, more closely related to sound and quite independent of syntactic structure, such as the system of representation now called "phonemic". However, as I will attempt to show below, the existence of an additional level is highly dubious, and for this reason

[7] It is instructive, in this connection, to recall the controversies aroused by Bloomfield's *Language*. In particular, Kent's review (1934) criticized it from the point of view of traditional (systematic) phonetics. Kent argues that "the difference between [s] and [š] is functional in English: shall we disregard it in citing Japanese, because it is not functional – even though we have the machinery for marking the distinction". In this vein, he criticizes Bloomfield's phonemicization of "secretary" [sekriterij] as /sekretejrij/ (which Bloomfield justifies, presumably, by reference to "secretarial" [sekritejrijil)], etc. In responding to the review, Bolling (1934) comments that to mark predictable phonetic variants, in particular, reduced variants of unstressed vowels, "would be like the meaningless underlining of a schoolgirl"; and he supports Bloomfield's phonemicizations by the argument that they mark only what is not predictable. It is interesting to note that the position that Bolling is attacking is, on many points, just the one that is adopted by the "neo-Bloomfieldian" linguists of the 1940's and 1950's, who characteristically criticize Bloomfield for failure to separate levels, and who return to a much "narrower" transcription. In particular, the marking of reduced variants of unstressed vowels is considered one of the major innovations in this development. We return to this issue directly.
The controversy between Kent and Bloomfield-Bolling concerns the choice between systematic phonetics and systematic phonemics. But it is clear that these are not alternatives, and that in fact both levels are significant in the description of a language. It was Bloomfield's summary rejection of phonetics as without scientific value or status, rather than his development of a higher level of representation, that should really have been at issue here.

I have preferred to keep the older term, modified by "systematic" to avoid confusion.

In general, we can say, with Palmer (1958), that the place of the phonological component is "that of an ancillary technique; it provides a bridge between the grammatical statement and the direct observations that are reported in phonetics". For linguistic theory, the significant questions concerning the phonological component have to do with the choice of phonetic features (and, more generally, the universal phonetic theory), and with the conditions on the form and ordering of rules. The latter question, in particular, is of great importance, and phonological theory has suffered seriously from its neglect. As soon as the attempt to construct explicit rules to determine the phonetic shape of a string of formatives passes the most superficial and introductory stage, it becomes obvious that a fairly strict ordering must be imposed on phonological processes, if they are to be describable in full generality. Thus most of the examples in Sapir (1933) involve ordering, though he does not explicitly mention this fact. Bloomfield was much concerned with questions of ordering[8] and his Menomini morphophonemics (1939) is the first modern example of a segment of a generative grammar with ordered rules. Bloomfield does not discuss the extent or depth of ordering in this grammar, and it is not easy to determine this from the examples that he gives. It apparently does not exceed five

---

[8]   Cf. Bloomfield (1933, 213). He regarded ordering of rules as an artifact – an invention of the linguist – as compared with order of constituents, which is "part of language". But this depreciation of the role of order of synchronic processes is just one aspect of the general antipathy to theory (the so-called "anti-mentalism") that Bloomfield developed and bequeathed to modern linguistics. This tendency fitted well with the operationalism, verificationism and behaviorism that formed a dominant intellectual mood in the early 1930's. Harris showed (1951a, 237) that some of Bloomfield's examples of ordering can be handled by unordered rules that state the phonemic composition of a morphophoneme *in a strictly morphophonemic context*. But his method does not generalize to such examples as the one given directly below; and, furthermore, it is not clear whether the italicized condition on morphophonemic rules is compatible with the procedures by which they are established, since these procedures set up morphophonemes (similarly, phonemes) in terms of phonemic (respectively, phonetic) or mixed environments. There are important questions of principle here that have not been sufficiently clarified.

(cf. Bever, 1963). In the segment of the phonological component for Modern Hebrew presented in Chomsky (1951), a depth of ordering that reaches the range of twenty to thirty is demonstrated[9] and this is surely an underestimate. Recent work (see note 5, p. 65) gives strong support to the belief that ordering relations among phonological processes are quite strict; and, furthermore, it provides evidence that the ordering is not strictly linear, but is in part cyclic (see § 1). Resolution of these questions seems to me the outstanding problem for contemporary phonology. Although several cases of ordering will be presented below, it is important to bear in mind that scattered examples cannot give an accurate indication of the extent or significance of ordering in a full grammar.

To make the discussion somwehat more concrete, consider the following simple example from English. We find such phonological regularities as the following (where the notation $[s_1, s_2]$ is used for the "archiphoneme" consisting of the features common to s_1, s_2)[10]

(20) (i) $\begin{Bmatrix} k \\ \\ t \end{Bmatrix} \rightarrow$ s in the context: $-\; +\; [i, y]$

(ii) $[s,z] + [i,y] \rightarrow [š,ž]$ in the context: $-$ Vowel.

Thus we have "opaque" – –opacity", "logic" – "logicism", "democrat" – "democracy", "pirate" – "piracy", in case (i); "race" – "racial", "express" – "expression", "erase" – "erasure", "enclose" – "enclosure", "revise" – "revision", in case (ii). Although various qualifications are needed, clearly rules such as these belong to English grammar. But if these are regarded as purely classificatory,

---

[9]   That is, it is shown that a sequence of some twenty-five rules can be formed such that any interchange of adjacent rules will lead to a reformulation that increases complexity (and hence reduces generality). In the light of more recent work, the grammar presented there would have to be modified in many respects, but the conclusion concerning ordering, so it appears, would, if anything, be strengthened.

[10]   A natural evaluation measure ("simplicity" measure) for the phonological component (cf. Halle, 1961a) is the number of feature specifications it contains. In particular, then, the grammar is more highly valued (and more general) if rules are stated in terms of archiphonemes (and, furthermore, "generalized archiphonemes" such as C, V, etc.) rather than segments.

unordered rules to the effect that "morphophoneme" X has the "phoneme" Y as member (or realization, etc.) in the context Z–W, then they must be supplemented by the additional rule

$$(21) \quad \begin{Bmatrix} k \\ \\ t \end{Bmatrix} + [i,y] \rightarrow š \text{ in the context}: - \text{Vowel},$$

to account for "logician", "delicious" (cf. "delicacy"), "relate" – "relation", "ignite" – "ignition", etc. But clearly this rule is unnecessary if (20ii) can apply to the result of application of (20i), that is, if the rules are ordered as in (20).

The grammar containing just (20i), (20ii), in that order, will provide such derivations as[11]

(22) lajik + yin   prezident + i   prezident + i + æl
     lajis + yin   prezidens + i   prezidens + i + æ (by (20i))
     lajišin   prezidenš + æl   (ƀy (20ii))

The top line in (22) is the systematic phonemic representation, in each case, and the last line becomes the systematic phonetic by additional rules. But none of the intermediate stages has any systematic status at all, apparently. For each linguistic form, the number of intermediate representations will depend on the number of rules in the ordered sequence that apply to it, and this number will differ for different forms, indeed, for different subparts of the same sentence, phrase, or word.

Clearly a grammar that contains (21) as a rule is missing a generalization. In fact, consideration of additional examples shows immediately that several generalizations are being missed. Thus observe that alongside of (20) there is also the rule

(23) z → s in the context: – + iv,

as in "abuse" – "abusive". But consider the forms "persuade" – "persuasive" – "persuasion", "corrode" – "corrosive" – "corrosion",

---

[11] As throughout, irrelevant details are omitted. In particular, for reasons beyond the scope of this discussion, the first vowel in "logic" should actually be not /a/ but the archiphoneme [ǎ, ǒ] (cf. note 19 on p. 90), and /i/ should actually be the "archiphoneme" lax vowel.

etc. In a taxonomic grammar with no provision for applying rules in sequences, these regularities must be accounted for by two entirely new rules, independent of (20), (21), (23), namely:

(24) (i) d → s in the context: - + iv

(ii) d + [i,y] → ž in the context: - Vowel.

If we allow rules to apply in sequence, the rules (24) are entirely superfluous. It is simply necessary to generalize (20i) to apply to [d,t] instead of simply /t/,[12] thus giving for "persuasive" the derivation (25) and for "persuasion" the derivation (26):

(25) perswēd + iv, perswēz + iv (by (20i)), perswēsiv (by (23))

(26) perswēd + yin, perswēz + yin (by (20i)), perswēžin (by (20ii)),

where again the first is the systematic phonemic and the last the systematic phonetic representation (details omitted).

Again, it is obvious that a grammar that accounts for this variety of phonetic facts by the rules (20) (suitably generalized) and (23), which are independently motivated, is much to be preferred, on grounds of descriptive adequacy, to one which contains in addition the rules (21), (24). The latter grammar is simply leaving significant generalizations unexpressed. But a descriptively adequate grammar in this case again requires that the rules be applied in the sequence given.

Finally, let us extend the analysis to include the forms (27), illustrating a point to which we will return below:

(27) (i)   decide [dīsaˑyd]

(ii) decided [dīsaˑyDɨd] - [D] = alveolar flap

(iii) decisive [dīsaysiv]

(iv) delight [dīlayt]

(v)   delighted [dīlayDɨd].

To account for such facts as these, we must add to the phonological

[12]   To this extent, this adjustment of (20i) simplifies the grammar (cf. note 10). Several qualifications are needed, however, which make the effect of the adjustment neutral, as regards complexity. Note that these rules should properly be stated strictly in terms of features. Thus, for example, rule (23) should assert, simply: [+ Continuant] → [- Voiced] in the context: - + iv.

component containing the rules (20) and (23), the rules (28) and (29), where the order is now: (20i), (20ii), (23), (28), (29).

(28) a →a· in the context: – (Glide) Voiced
(29) [t,d] → D in the context: Stressed Vowel – Unstressed Vocalic.

Again, these can be generalized in familiar ways, and each is required, independently, by many other examples. With the rules so ordered we have such derivations as the following:

(30)	*decide*	*decided*	*decisive*	*delight*	*delighted*	*Rule*
(a)	dīsayd	dīsayd≠d	dīsayd+iv	dīlayt	dīlayt≠d	
(b)	dīsayd	dīsayd≠d	dīsayz+iv	dīlayt	dīlayt≠d	(20i)
(c)	dīsayd	dīsayd≠d	dīsays+iv	dīlayt	dīlayt≠d	(23)
(d)	dīsa·yd	dīsa·yd≠d	dīsays+iv	dīlayt	dīlayt≠d	(28)
(e)	dīsa·yd	dīsa·ydɨd	dīsays+iv	dīlayt	dīlaytɨd	
(f)	dīsa·yd	dīsa·yDɨd	dīsays+iv	dīlayt	dīlayDɨd	(29)

Again details and well-known rules are omitted. Line (a) is the systematic phonemic and line (f) the systematic phonetic representation. At no other stage does the set of representations have any systematic character that I can detect. Perhaps (c) is what would be called "phonemic" by many structural linguists (though not, e.g., by Bloch). If so, it is to be observed that ordering of rules is also necessary to convert the "phonemic" representation to the phonetic one, in the optimal way, since clearly if (28) and (29) are not given in this order, the correct output will not be achieved. Thus the [D] of "delighted" is phonetically voiced, but is functionally Voiceless, for the application of rule (28) – thus it has the classificatory distinctive feature of Voicelessness and the phonetic feature of Voiced, in the framework proposed above.

As we enlarge the range of examples considered, the depth of required ordering increases (as does its intricacy, when we introduce the transformational cycle). Investigation of this question has, so far, failed to reveal any systematic set of representations that might be taken as constituting a level of representation at any intermediate point in the operation of the phonological component, and therefore it seems necessary to conclude that systematic phonemics and systematic phonetics are the only two levels of representation that appear in structural descriptions provided by the phonological component. To fortify this conclusion, I would like to consider briefly the status of modern taxonomic phonemics, as seen from this point of view.

4.3. TAXONOMIC PHONEMICS

Sound pattern has been taken as the primary object of study in modern, structural linguistics; it has, furthermore, been studied in relative or complete isolation from the syntactic setting within which phonological processes operate.[13] In both of these respects, structural linguistics marks a departure from a more traditional point of view, which again emerges in recent work in generative grammar, as sketched above. Though modern phonologists have not achieved anything like unanimity, a body of doctrine has emerged to all or part of which a great many linguists would subscribe. Abstracting away from much variation, let us coin the term "taxonomic phonemics" to refer to this body of doctrine, thus emphasizing its striking reliance, in almost all versions, on procedures of segmentation and classification (identification of variants).

Taxonomic phonemic theory constitutes the first attempt to formulate a linguistic theory with sufficient clarity and care so that questions of theoretical adequacy can seriously be raised. The development of taxonomic phonemics has led to standards of explicitness and precision that had rarely been attained in previous linguistic description, and to many new insights into sound structure.

---

[13] I naturally cannot hope to survey all contemporary points of view in the space of this paper, and I will concentrate on those that seem to me the clearest, referring to Troubetzkoy, Harris, Bloch and Jakobson, among others. I will not consider glossematics (which, for reasons unclear to me, is often referred to as extremely rigorous and of high "operational preciseness" – cf., e.g., Haugen, 1951; Diderichsen, 1958), or the prosodic analysis of the London school, since I have been unable to find formulations of these positions that are explicit enough to show what evidence might count either for or against them, though the latter, in particular seems to have certain relations to the point of view sketched above in § 4.2. See Langendoen (1964) for a discussion of prosodic analysis, and an interpretation of its results within a framework of the kind proposed here.

Furthermore, the period of its dominance has also been one of unparalleled extension of the range of linguistic investigation. For these reasons, the methodological and substantive assumptions that underlie this theory deserve careful and critical scrutiny. It seems to me, however, that they have not received the kind of critical appraisal that this position merits. In this discussion of taxonomic phonemics, I will attempt to show that several of the major methodological and substantive assumptions that have played a crucial role in taxonomic phonemics are invalid, and that, in several important respects, the theory of taxonomic phonemics, as it has emerged during the last thirty years, is less adequate than the phonemic theory that was implicit in the work of such pioneers of modern phonology as, for example, Edward Sapir.

Under discussion, then, are four potential levels of representation associated with the phonological component, namely, the levels of:

(31) (i)   physical phonetics
     (ii) systematic phonetics
     (iii) taxonomic phonemics
     (iv) systematic phonemics

Physical phonetics is the study referred to by Troubetzkoy (1939) as "the science of the sounds of *parole*", a study with methods and goals entirely different from those of phonology (the "science of the sounds of *langue*"). It provides Bloomfield's "mechanical record of the gross acoustic features, such as is produced in the phonetics laboratory" (1933, 85); its status is not in question here, and no further attention will be given to it.

I will assume, for the purposes of this discussion, that the status of systematic phonemics ("morphophonemics", in one sense of the more usual modern phrase) is also not in question.

The status of systematic phonetics and the condition of phonetic specifiability (cf. p. 67, above), however, has been very much in question, and it has, in fact, been explicitly repudiated in many theoretical discussions. Thus for Bloomfield (1933, 85), the only kind of linguistic record that is "scientifically relevant", aside from that provided by physical phonetics, "is a record in terms of pho-

nemes, ignoring all features that are not distinctive in the language".
Phonetic transcription is dismissed as haphazard, limitless, accidental, and of no scientific value; and Bloomfield maintains that
in phonology "we pay no heed to the acoustic nature of phonemes
but merely accept them as distinct units and study their distribution" (p. 137). Troubetzkoy sometimes refers to phonemes as
completely "abstract" units serving only a distinctive function.
But elsewhere, he pays a great deal of attention to the systematiza-
tion of the universal phonetic features that play a distinctive role
in some language (structural phonetics – cf. 1939, 93f.). Bloomfield's apparent rejection of the level of structural phonetics re-
appears in an extreme form in Joos' (1957) summary of what he
takes to be the characteristic view of American linguistics, namely,
that "languages could differ from each other without limit and in
unpredictable ways" (96), that "distinctive features are established
ad hoc for each language or even dialect", and that "no universal
theory of segments can be called upon to settle the moot points"
(228). Similarly, Hjelmslev appears to deny the relevance of phonetic substance to phonological representation.

Nevertheless, it seems to me correct to regard modern taxonomic
phonemics, of all varieties, as resting squarely on assumptions concerning a universal phonetic theory of the sort described above.
Analysis of actual practice shows no exceptions to the reliance on
phonetic universals. No procedure has been offered to show why,
for example, initial [pʰ] should be identified with final [p] rather
than final [t], in English, that does not rely essentially on the assumption that the familiar phonetic properties (Stop, Labial, etc.)
are the "natural" ones. Harris might be interpreted as suggesting
that a non-phonetic principle can replace reliance an absolute
phonetic properties when he concludes (1951a, 66) that "simplicity
of statement, as well as phonetic similarity, decide in favor of the
p-pʰ grouping"; but this implication, if intended, is surely false.
The correct analysis is simpler only if we utilize the familiar
phonetic properties for phonetic specification. With freedom of
choice of features, any arbitrary grouping may be made simpler.
From innumerable examples of this sort, it seems that we must con-

LIBRARY ST. MARY'S COLLEGE

clude that, despite disclaimers, all varieties of taxonomic phonemics rely essentially on the condition of phonetic specifiability. Furthermore, actual practice shows remarkable agreement as to which features constitute the universal phonetic system that is implicitly assumed.

It appears, then, that the status of systematic phonetics is also beyond dispute, though there is room for much discussion as to what is the actual character of the universal phonetic theory that underlies all descriptive practice. In any event, we can assume that each utterance of any language can be uniquely represented as a sequence of *phones*, each of which can be regarded as an abbreviation for a set of features (those that constitute the universal theory in question), in terms of which "phonetic similarity", "simplicity of statement", "pattern congruity", and so on, are defined.

Let us turn then to a more detailed investigation of taxonomic phonemics, taking this to be a theory that requires that phonological representations must, in addition to the condition of phonetic specifiability, meet conditions which, for the sake of this discussion, I will designate by the following terms:

(32) (i)   linearity
     (ii) invariance
     (iii) biuniqueness
     (iv) local determinacy.

The linearity condition (32i) requires that each occurrence of a phoneme in the phonemic representation of an utterance be associated with a particular succession of (one or more) consecutive phones in its representing matrix, as its "member" or "realization"; and, furthermore, that if A precedes B in the phonemic representation, then the phone sequence associated with A precedes (is to the left of) that associated with B in the phonetic matrix. This condition follows from definitions of the phoneme as a class of phone sequences (as in post-Bloomfieldian American linguistics, typically[14] or as a bundle of distinctive features (Bloomfield, Jakobson) or a minimal term in a phonological opposition (Prague circle).

[14] In the case of Bloch's very careful system of definitions (cf. Bloch, 1950,

The invariance condition (32ii) asserts that each phoneme P has associated with it a certain set $\varphi(P)$ of *defining features* (that is, P = Q if and only if $\varphi(P) = \varphi(Q)$) and that wherever P occurs in a phonemic representation, there is an associated occurrence of $\varphi(P)$ in the corresponding phonetic representation. The invariance condition has no clear meaning unless the linearity condition is also met; I will assume, then, that it is inapplicable when linearity is violated. The invariance condition, in the form stated above, is required explicitly by Bloomfield, Troubetzkoy, Jakobson and Bloch, for example, and appears to be implicit in many other conceptions. Where linearity and invariance are both met by a taxonomic phonemic representation, the string of phones is segmented into successive segments, each of which contains, along with redundant (determined) features, the defining features $\varphi(P)$ of some phoneme P, and the phonemic representation is just the sequence of these phonemes.

One can distinguish two versions of the invariance condition, depending on whether the features are taken to be *relative* (i.e., more or less along a certain phonetic dimension) or *absolute*. Jakobson explicitly accepts the relative version of the invariance condition, and Bloch, as I understand his account, seems to accept

---

for a lucid sketch), the linearity condition is not necessarily met, but it is met, apparently, insofar as linear order is defined on phonemes at all. There are various unclarities here, despite the care of Bloch's presentation. Thus as the definitions stand, it is impossible for English [pʰ] to be a member of the phoneme /p/ (with [p]), since the defining qualities for /p/ are not coextensive with [pʰ] (or if a defining quality need qualify only part of a phone, it would follow that, e.g., [sp] could be assigned to /p/ and to /s/). It is also unclear what is meant by the statement that the phonemes of a dialect must "accomodate all the phones". Thus English "solely" has a doubled [l], phonetically. By definition, this pair of successive segments constitutes a phone. Must this phone be a member of a phoneme, or can the phonemic representation have two /l/'s, given the requirement that the phonemes must accommodate the phones? Bloch's work illustrates an important point, namely, that as the explicitness of formulation of taxonomic phonemics increases, the difficulty of giving a consistent and descriptively adequate interpretation also increases. Thus as compared with the other phonemic theories under consideration here, Bloch's is quite explicit; but the difficulty of determining whether the conditions (32) are met is at least as great in the case of his phonological theory as in the case of the others.

the absolute version. Under the absolute invariance condition, partial overlapping is excluded. If a certain occurrence of a phone P is assigned to a phoneme Q, then every other occurrence of P must be assigned to Q. Under the relative version of the invariance condition, certain cases of partial overlapping are permissible.

There are, however, some unresolved conceptual difficulties concerning the formulation of the relative invariance condition. Consider, e.g., a binary feature F such that a phone P in a certain context X-Y is assigned the feature [+F] or [–F] depending on its relation, in terms of the feature F, to some other phone Q in the context X-Y. But how is the context X-Y in question to be specified? If in terms of phones, then in general we can expect that the contrasting element Q will not appear in the context X-Y, but in a context X'-Y', where X' belongs to the same phoneme as X and Y' to the same phoneme as Y. If in terms of phonemes, then what happens when features that define X and Y are again relative to a context which, in this case, includes P and Q? For some discussion, see Chomsky (1957b).

Technically, the biuniqueness condition (32iii) asserts that each sequence of phones is represented by a unique sequence of phonemes, and that each sequence of phonemes represents a unique sequence of phones.[15] The biuniqueness condition is very widely maintained by modern phonologists, in particular, by those mentioned above. However, it is very difficult to formulate this condition in a manner that is actually in accord with their intentions. Consider, for example, Hockett's explicit discussion of it (1951). He considers a hypothetical language with no morphophonemic contrast between voiced and voiceless stops and with the rule:

(33) Stop → Voiced, medially, in words.

Thus morphophonemic pat#atak becomes phonetic [patadak], while morphophonemic patat#ak becomes phonetic [padatak]. But, Hockett argues, if we hear [padatak] we do not know whether

---

[15] In this form, the condition is of course rarely met. What is intended, rather, is that each sequence of phonemes represents a sequence of phones that is unique up to free variation.

to transcribe /patat#ak/ or /pata#tak/. Consequently the morphophonemic representation fails the biuniqueness condition, and cannot be taken as the phonemic representation, which, in this case, must mark the distinction between voiced and voiceless consonants. This illustrative example, however, leaves many questions unanswered. Suppose, following Hockett, "that there is no word /pada/, or no word /tak/, or that, both of these words existing, they would not occur in this sequence". Or, suppose that there is a general rule to the effect that no word ends in a vowel. In any such case, "we can conclude that the proper representation would be *patat ak*" (/patat#ak/), and the morphophonemic representation would, technically, meet the biuniqueness condition and would thus qualify as phonemic, if we take this condition literally.

Hockett does not state whether he would accept this system as phonemic, in this case, but it is fairly clear from the context that he would not. In fact, a decision to accept it as phonemic would seem to be inconsistent with his principle of separation of levels, to which we return below, under any reasonable interpretation of this. It is fairly clear that linguists who accept the so-called biuniqueness condition would regard the situation just described as still being a violation of "biuniqueness" in the intended sense. That is, they do not mean by "biuniqueness" simply one-one correspondence, but rather a correspondence such that the unique phonemic representation corresponding to a given phonetic form can be determined by "purely phonetic" considerations, or perhaps, considerations involving only "neighboring sounds". This convention, which is rather difficult to state precisely, is what I have called the condition of local determinacy (32iv). Apparently it is this, rather than literal biuniqueness in the technical sense, that is required in taxonomic phonemics.

Notice that from the linearity and absolute invariance condition one can deduce a particularly strong form of the biuniqueness and local determinacy conditions, namely, as noted above, the condition that the phoneme corresponding to a particular phone can be determined independently of the context of this phone. That is, even partial overlapping is disallowed, and (32iv) is vacuous.

Although, as noted above, the situation is still some what confused in the case of the relative invariance condition, it is clear that proponents of such positions (e.g., Jakobson, Harris) would disallow complete overlapping but not partial overlapping, since however they interpret the invariance condition, they do insist on some sort of "biuniqueness".

Although conditions (32i-iv) are (with a qualification to which I return below in § 4.3) quite generally accepted, and though they do follow from familiar definitions of the phoneme, there are many examples showing that they are untenable. Consider first the linearity condition. Of the many examples that illustrate its incorrectness,[16] perhaps the simplest is one presented in a recent paper by Malécot (1960). He observes that Lax Vowel + Nasal is often realized as Nasalized Vowel before Unvoiced Stop, in English, so that e.g., phonemic /kænt/ is phonetic [kæ̃t], though phonemic /hænd/ is phonetic [hæ̃nd]. In the face of this evidence, no linguist would conclude that vowel nasalization is distinctive in English, and that "can't" – "cat" constitute a minimal pair, while "can't" – "canned" do not. Rather, in such a case, the linearity condition would be disregarded. Furthermore, there can be no doubt that this decision is correct. The phonetic representation can be derived from the phonemic, in this case, by the phonetic rules (34), ordered as given:

(34) (i) Vowel → Nasalized in the context: – Nasal + Consonant
     (ii) Nasal → Ø in the context: Lax Vowel – Unvoiced Stop.

Though perfectly general and straightforward, these rules happen to lead to a violation of the linearity condition.

A second and more extreme example of the violation of linearity is the case of the a-a· contrast, discussed above (p. 74, § 4.2). The rules (28), (29), applied in this order, convert the systematic pho--nemic representations of row (I) of (35) first to row (II) and then to the systematic phonetic representation of row (III):

(35) (I)   rayt#r   rayd#r   ("writer", "rider", respectively)
     (II)   rayt#r   ra·yd#r   (by (28))

---

[16]   For several, see Harris (1951a, chapters 7,9).

(III)   rayDɨr   ra·yDɨr   (by (29), etc.)

But here words which differ phonemically only in their fourth segments differ phonetically only in their second segments. Hence if phonemic representation is to play any significant role in linguistic description (if it is to be part of a grammar that achieves descriptive adequacy), the linearity condition must be rather grossly violated.

These violations of the linearity condition incidentally show, in yet another way,[17] the incorrectness of the claim that phonology can (or, even more unaccountably, that it must) be based on sy-

[17] For further discussion, see Chomsky (1957a). Notice, for example, that such a pair as [r], [D] are in free variation and are assigned to the same phoneme in the context /θ-Vowel/ ("three", "throw", etc.) in many English dialects, but replacement of one by the other in /bæ-l/ leads to a meaning difference ("battle", "barrel") (whereas, on the other hand, /t/ and /d/ can replace one another in the context /bɨrn-/ ("burned", "burnt") with no change in meaning, though they would never be assigned to the same phoneme), so that the semantic criterion is falsified from right to left. And [ə], [r], though phonetically similar, clearly cannot be assigned to the same phoneme (cf. below) though they never contrast (with or without change of meaning), so that the criterion is falsified from left to right.

The history of the notion "contrast" in modern linguistics is very curious. Bloomfield (1926) took it as a primitive notion, and Harris provided a fairly effective operational test (1951a, 32f.), which is the only known device that can be used when the problem of determining contrast actually arises in practice. The only coherent attempt to define "contrast" has been Bloch's careful distributional definition. This has been frequently criticized, mainly on grounds of impracticality. Insofar as the criticism is valid, it shows only that "contrast" must be taken as a primitive notion. However, the criticism has almost universally been taken as showing that "contrast" must be defined in terms of "synonymy of utterance tokens" (e.g., Diderichsen, 1958), and in the background of the entire development has been the assumption that there is such a definition. Obviously, however, difficulties in one analysis do not show that another analysis is correct. And in fact there is no proposal for defining "contrast" in terms of "synonymy" that does not have obvious objections to it. In fact, the only definition I have been able to find or to construct that does not immediately fail (Chomsky, 1957a, 96–5) not only requires (with Bloch) that each token appear in each possible context, but that it occur in each possible context with each "meaning", so that the "impracticality" of Bloch's proposal is compounded many-fold. Perhaps some semantic criterion for "contrast" exists. This we will not know, however, until proponents of this view take the same care in formulating their proposal as Bloch did in formulating his. Until such time, it can only be dismissed as a totally unsupported claim.

nonymy, in its usual formulation to the effect that phonetically similar sounds are not assigned to the same phoneme if and only if replacement of one by the other in some context leads to a change of meaning (cf., e.g., Diderichsen, 1949). If what is meant by "context" is "phonetic context" then the criterion would give the result that V-Ṽ and a-a· constitute a phonological opposition (contrast) in English. If what is meant is "phonemic context", then obviously the question at issue is simply being begged. In general, it should be observed that "minimal pair" is not an elementary notion. It cannot, in any interesting sense, be defined in phonetic terms, but only in terms of a completed phonemic analysis. Consequently, the "commutation test" is of little significance if formulated, in the usual manner, as a procedure for phonemic analysis.

Such violations of the linearity condition have not gone unnoticed by careful taxonomic phonologists, and it is instructive to consider the steps that have been taken to meet them. Troubetzkoy gives an example quite analogous to (34) both in the *Anleitung* and the *Grundzüge* (1939, 46). He observes that the following phonological rules operate in Russian:

(36) (i) o → ǫ in the context: – l
     (ii) l → Ø in the context: Vowel – Nasal + Consonant.

Thus phonemic /sólncǎ/ ("sun") is phonetic [sǫ́ncə], and there is no necessity to set up /ǫ/ in contrast to /o/ as a new phoneme. Here the linearity condition is violated, as in (34); and, furthermore, the rules must be ordered as given. To account for such violations of linearity, Troubetzkoy proposes a general rule for phonemicization which we can state as follows:

(37) If the phone A is phonetically similar to the phone sequence BC, and A-BC are in free variation or complementary distribution, and BC is a realization of the phoneme sequence PQ, then A is to be regarded as a realization of PQ.

Thus [ǫ] is phonetically similar to and in complementary distribution with [ǫl], which is a realization of /ol/; thus [ǫ] is a realization of /ol/.[18] Similarly, nasalized vowels, in some English dialects, are in complementary distribution with Vowel + Nasal, and could thus be regarded as a realization of Vowel + Nasal, thus dealing with the violation of linearity caused by (34), in these dialects. Similarly, one might use the same argument to justify representing inter-vocalic and word final English [ŋ] as /ng/ (though to apply the argument in this case, complementary distribution would have to be defined in terms of phonemically specified, rather than phonetically specified contexts).

However, the rule (37) seems to me not at all satisfying. It is entirely ad hoc, and it can only be taken as indicating that the definition of the phoneme as a minimal term of a phonological opposition is incorrect. More seriously, it cannot be applied in general, without absurdity. Thus, in English, the pairs [n̩]-[ny], [yŭ]-[y] are phonetically similar and in complementary distribution, but it would be absurd, following the rule, to phonemicize [kitn̩] ("kitten") as /kitny/ or [yat] ("yacht") as /yŭat/. Even more serious for the taxonomic phonemicist, is the fact that this rule can lead to a violation of biuniqueness. Thus consider the English [ă]-[aˑ] contrast ("write" – "ride"), discussed above. [ăy] appears only initially or after a consonant, and before an unvoiced consonant; [y] can never appear in this position. Since [y] and [ăy] are phone-tically similar and [ăy] is a realization of /ay/, by Troubetzkoy's rule, [y] is a realization of /ay/. Aside from the absurdity, this leads to a violation of biuniqueness, in this case, since /y/ and /ay/ contrast ("ion" /ayan/ – "yon" /yan/). Hence aside from being ad hoc, this rule cannot be regarded as an extension of the notion "phoneme" to deal with the case of violation of linearity.

Troubetzkoy's informal comments and discussion of examples indicate that the rule, as he stated it, perhaps does not conform to his actual intentions. Suppose, in fact, that we were to restrict application of the rule (37) to the case in which B is a Lax Vowel and C a Liquid or Nasal. Then the violations of linearity in the Russian example (36) and the English example (34) (but not the

---

[18]   Note that Troubetzkoy's rule must be modified, for adequacy, since as it stands it would require that [ọl] be regarded as a realization of /oll/.

example of English /ng/) would still be handled, while the counter-examples of the preceding paragraph would be ruled out. But now the entirely ad hoc character of the rule becomes even more clear, and surely with such a restrictive formulation as this no one would seriously regard it as constituting part of the definition of the fundamental concept "phoneme". Furthermore, it is still not difficult to construct counter-examples. Thus in many American dialects, [e] of "get" is in complementary distribution with [ɛr] of "berry", which is a realization of /er/; so that by the rule, even as amended, [e] must be regarded as a realization of /er/, and "get" must be phonemicized /gert/.

The rule (37) is a typical example of an ad hoc device invented to remedy an inadequacy of some general notion of "taxonomic phoneme", and this discussion of difficulties that it faces could be duplicated for other principles of this sort. These ad hoc revisions of a basically inadequate notion do not succeed in reaching the central issue. In such cases as those discussed above, it is clear that the acceptability of an analysis hinges on its effect on the grammar as a whole. Thus the rules (34i) and (34ii) are quite general and are independently motivated. A grammar that incorporates them is materially simpler than one that does not. But the rules: /yu/ → [y] before Vowels, or /er/ → [e] before Consonants, as in the absurd examples given above, obviously do not simplify the grammar of English. Similarly, Troubetzkoy's Russian example is well-motivated by general systematic considerations; e.g., by the existence of such forms as /sólnešnij/, [sǫ́ln,išnij], and by the fact that were (36) not incorporated in the grammar, then each occurrence of /o/ in the lexicon would have to be marked as distinct from /ǫ/, greatly complicating the grammar (cf. note 10). Similarly, the necessity of assigning English [ŋ] to /n/ (more accurately, to the archiphoneme Nasal) becomes obvious only when the full range of examples involving Nasal + Stop in various syntactic positions comes under investigation. The fact that considerations of this sort are crucial suggests that any such "atomistic" rule as the one that Troubetzkoy suggests will fail.

General systematic considerations are, however, foreign to the point of view of taxonomic phonemics, and, in fact, they have often been criticized as circular (cf., e.g., Twaddell, 1935, 66). This criticism is correct, given the general "procedural" bias of modern phonology; but it shows only that the attempt to develop a taxonomic phonemics on the basis of analytic procedures of segmentation and classification, supplemented by such ad hoc rules as (37), is ill-conceived from the start.

The more extreme case of violation of linearity posed by "writer" – "rider" (which is beyond the range of (37) or any modification of it) is discussed by Harris (1951a, 70). He proposes that [ayD] be assigned to /ayt/ as a unit, and [a·yD] to /ayd/ as a unit, on general grounds of symmetry of distribution. But this is a rather vague notion, and it is not at all clear how it would fare once clarified. Furthermore, suppose that somehow a criterion of distributional symmetry can be formulated that has just the desired effect in this case. This result would still seem to be accidental and beside the point, since clearly in this case the critical factors are, once again, the generality and independent motivation of the rules (28), (29), and the relation of the forms in question to others; in particular, the relation of "writer" to "write" and "rider" to "ride", which would surely be expressed, on syntactic grounds, in the systematic phonemic representation. But these factors have nothing directly to do with distributional symmetry. They are, once again, of a general systematic character, and thus lie beyond the narrow scope of taxonomic phonemics. Finally, notice that Harris' proposal appears to involve an inconsistency with respect to the notion "distribution". Phonemes are to be established in purely distributional terms. If the distribution is with respect to *phonetic* contexts, then the definition of "phoneme" is violated by his assignment of [a] and [a·] to /a/, since these phones contrast in the phonetic context [—yD]. If the distribution is with respect to *phonemic* contexts (an assumption difficult to reconcile with a procedural approach, as noted above), then the definition is violated by the assignment of [D] to either /t/ or /d/, depending on the phonetic context, in this case.

It seems to me, then, that the ad hoc devices for dealing with the

violations of linearity are not defensible, and that the definition of a
phoneme as "a bundle of [phonetic] distinctive features", "a class
of phones in free variation or complementary distribution", or a
"minimal term in a phonological opposition" can be maintained
only if we are willing to tolerate such absurdities as the phonemic
representations /kæt/, /rayDɨr/, /raˑyDɨr/ for "can't", "writer",
"rider", and so on, in many other cases.

Consider now the invariance condition. Notice first that it fails
in the case of violations of linearity such as those discussed above.
However, it seems to me untenable even when linearity is preserved. Phonemic overlapping provides the clearest example of this.
Thus consider an English dialect in which [D] is the allophone of
/r/ in "throw" and of /t/ in "Betty" (where it contrasts with the /r/
of "berry" – cf. Bloch, 1941). Following the principle of invariance,
we must assign [D] to /t/ in the context $\neq\theta$-, counter not only to
the speaker's intuition but also to the otherwise valid rules of consonant distribution. The situation is worse in dialects in which [D]
and [r] are in free variation in this context and in intervocalic
contrast, in which case no coherent solution is possible within the
framework of (32), although the description of the facts is perfectly
straightforward. The situation is still worse if we accept the absolute invariance condition, particularly if (as in Bloch, 1950) the
features ("qualities") are defined in auditory terms. For it is
known that in this case, not even the correct analysis of English
stops is tenable, since /p/, /t/ and /k/ overlap (Schatz, 1953). For
reasons such as these, then, it seems that the invariance condition
cannot be accepted, however the condition of linearity is treated.

The biuniqueness condition is difficult to discuss because of the
unclarity of formulation noted above. Nevertheless, certain con-
sequences of accepting it are clear, and it seems to me that these
are quite devastating, for anyone concerned with descriptive adequacy. Halle has pointed out that it is generally impossible to
provide a level of representation meeting the biuniqueness condition without destroying the generality of rules, when the sound
system has an asymmetry. Thus he gives the following, quite typical
example from Russian (Halle, 1959b). In (38) the four forms in

column I are given in systematic phonemic representation and in column III in systematic phonetic representation:

(38)

I	II	III
d'at, l,i	d'at, l,i	d'at, l,i
d'at, bi	d'ad, bi	d'ad, bi
ž'eč l,i	ž'eč l,i	ž'eč l,i
ž'eč bi	ž'eč bi	ž'ej bi

The forms of column III are produced from those of column I by the general rule:

(39) Obstruent → Voiced in the context: – Voiced Obstruent.

But the representations in column I fail the condition of biuniqueness as usually construed (in terms of local determinacy), and consequently would not be accepted as taxonomic phonemic. The representations in column II would be accepted as "phonemic" by taxonomic phonologists, because of the fact that t, - d, contrast while č - j do not. But if the grammar is to provide II as a level of representation, then it cannot incorporate the general rule (39), but must have in its place the two rules (40i) and (40ii), the first of which is taken as a rule relating "morphophonemic" to "phonemic" representation, and the second as relating "phonemic" to phonetic representation:

(40) (i) Obstruent → Voiced in the context: – Voiced Obstruent, except for c, č, x;

(ii) c, č, x → Voiced in the context: – Voiced Obstruent.

It seems to me that the force of this example has not been sufficiently appreciated by taxonomic phonemicists. Where it has been noted at all, the discussion has not been adequate. Ferguson, in his review (1962) of Halle (1959b), discusses not the example given in the book under review (and reproduced above), but instead a Turkish example that had at first been proposed by Lees as analogous to Halle's, and then withdrawn by Lees as inappropriate (Lees, 1961, p. 63). Insofar as Ferguson's discussion carries over to the correct example that Halle gives, it amounts only to the observation that from the phonetic record alone it is possible to determine the underlying systematic phonemic (in his terms, morphophonemic) form in the case of c, č, x, but not in the case of the other obstruents. This is correct but irrelevant, since this information is provided just as explicitly in the grammar which incorporates only systematic phonemics and systematic phonetics as in the grammar which, in addition, adds an intermediate level of taxonomic phonemics. Thus the fact remains that in this case, the only effect of assuming that there is a taxonomic phonemic level is to make it impossible to state the generalization.

In the face of Halle's example, I do not see how one can fail to be uncomfortable in attributing to Russian a level of taxonomic phonemics. Furthermore, similar examples are not difficult to find in other languages. Bloch, in fact, gave a rather similar example in his discussion of phonemic overlapping (Bloch, 1941). In his dialect of English there are forms that might have the systematic phonemic representations of column I and the systematic phonetic representations of column III of (41):

(41)   I   II   III
      "nod": nad   na·d   na·d
      "knot": nat   nat   nat
      "bed": bed   bed   be·d
      "bet": bet   bet   bet.

Column I does not meet the biuniqueness condition because of such contrasts as "balm" – "bomb", "starry" – "sorry", "father" – "bother", and because of the fact that the vowel of "Pa'd (do it)" is that of "pod", phonetically. Column III can be derived from column I by the familiar rule of lengthening before voiced segments (of which (28) is a special case).[19] But Bloch is forced, by the biuni-

---

[19]   This discussion is quite unaffected by the residual cases of a-a· contrast. For Bloch's dialect, "father", and "bother" have different vowels, quite independently of how we analyze the forms of (41). In fact, it is no accident that the short vowel in the a-a· pairs is generally spelled "o" while the long one is spelled "a". A good case can be made for the conclusion that the vowel phoneme of "nod", "knot", "bomb", etc., is actually [ă, ŏ], which in certain dialects goes to [a·] (merging with the variant of /a/), in others goes to [a] (giving the a-a· contrast), and in others becomes [ə]. This assumption is required by many other considerations, e.g., to describe in the most general way the familiar ē → æ

queness condition, to accept II as the phonemic level of representation. Thus a full grammar of English, meeting this condition,
would have to replace the general rule of vowel lengthening by two
rules, the first of which applies only to /a/ and the second to all
other vowels. The first would relate "morphophonemic" and
"phonemic", and the second "phonemic" and phonetic representations. The situation is exactly analogous to the Russian example
just given, and again we see that the effect of the biuniqueness condition is to complicate the grammar, that is, to prevent it from
achieving descriptive adequacy.

The complicating effect of the biuniqueness condition has been
commented on by several of its proponents. Thus Bloch remarks
at once, in discussing the preceding example, that it leads to a loss
of symmetry. Similarly, he remarks (1950, note 3) that the National
Romanization which influenced his earlier, non-biunique analysis
of Japanese, though "neat and systematic", is not as close to a
"phonemic notation" as the Hepburn Romanization, "unsystematic
and cumbersome as it seems to be". Similarly, Hockett (1951)
compares Bloch's "deceptively simple" non-biunique analysis with
his later "quite complicated ... but obviously more accurate"
taxonomic phonemic analysis. In fact, however, the "greater
accuracy" of the latter seems to reside in nothing other than its
observance of conditions (32i-iv). We return below to the question
of why this is regarded as a sign of greater accuracy.

We have, as yet, said nothing about the principle of complementary distribution, which is the central concept of taxonomic
phonemics as developed, for example, by Jones, Troubetzkoy,
Harris and Bloch. This principle is, basically, the principle of
biuniqueness converted into a procedure. Regarded as an analytic
procedure, its goal is to provide the minimally redundant representation meeting the conditions of biuniqueness and local determin-

---

and ō → a alternations. Cf. Halle and Chomsky (forthcoming) for a detailed
discussion. The issue is further complicated by dialects (cf. Sledd, 1959) in
which liquids drop pre-consonantaly (giving long variants of short vowels in
such words as "absolve" /æbsɔlv/ – cf., "absolution" – etc.). This is just one
of the many examples that show how wide a range of information is necessary
to determine what is in fact a minimal pair.

acy. We will show, however, that it is in general incapable of providing the minimally redundant analysis meeting these conditions, and furthermore, that it may even lead to a non-biunique analysis. We can formulate the principle in this way (following Harris, 1951a, chapter 7): Given a set of representations in terms of phones, let us define the distribution $D(x)$ of the phone x as the set of (short-range) phonetic contexts in which x occurs. The relation of complementary distribution holds between phones x and y if $D(x)$ and $D(y)$ have no element in common. A *tentative phoneme* is a class of phones related pair-wise by the relation of complementary distribution. Some would require further that a defining phonetic property be associated with each tentative phoneme, marking each of its members and no other phone (the invariance condition).[20] A *tentative phonemic system* is a family of tentative phonemes meeting a condition of exhaustiveness. We find *the* phonemic system (or systems) by applying additional criteria of symmetry.

But consider the example of phonemic overlapping due to Bloch that was discussed above, namely, the case of a dialect with [D] as the realization of /r/ in "throw" and of /t/ in "Betty", where it contrasts with the [r] of "berry". The requirement of biuniqueness is preserved if we set up the phonemes /t/, with the allophone [D] in intervocalic, post-stress position, and /r/, with the allophone [D] after dental spirants. Given a phone in a phonetic context, we can now uniquely assign it to a phoneme; and given a phoneme in a phonemic context we can uniquely determine its phonetic realization (up to free variation). However, this solution, which is the only reasonable one (and the one Bloch accepted in his 1941 paper), is inconsistent with the principle of complementary distribution. In fact, the allophones [D] and [r] of /r/ are not in complementary distribution, since they both occur in the context [be-iy] ("Betty", "berry"). Hence complementary distribution is not a necessary condition for biuniqueness. Furthermore, the class of "tentative

---

[20]   This would be required by Troubetzkoy, Jakobson and Bloch, but not by Harris (cf. 1951a, 72, note 28). He maintains that "any grouping of complementary segments may be called phonemic", and that further criteria have to do only with convenience, not with linguistic fact.

phonemic systems" as defined in the preceding paragraph will not include the optimal biunique system as a member, so that no supplementary criteria will suffice to select it from this class. But now observe further that the class of tentative phonemic systems, as defined, will contain systems that fail the principle of biuniqueness. Thus, for example, [k] and [ă] are in complementary distribution in English (and, furthermore, share features shared by nothing else, e.g., in Jakobson's terms, the features Compact, Grave, Lax, Non-Flat). Hence they qualify as a tentative phoneme, and there is a tentative phonemic system in which they are identified as members of the same phoneme /K/. But in this phonemic system, "socked" [săkt] and "Scot" [skăt] will both be represented phonemically as /sKKt/. Similarly, [ə] and [r] are in complementary distribution (and share defining features) and thus qualify as a potential phoneme. But if they are identified as variants of /R/, we will have "prevail" /pRRvēl/, [prəveyl], "pervade" /pRRvēd/ [pərveyd], which is a violation of local determinacy, and of biuniqueness as generally construed. Nor is adjacency a crucial feature of such counter-examples. Suppose, for example, that we set up the "phoneme" /D/ consisting of the allophones of /d/ and the pre-[r] allophone of /ĭ/, which are pair-wise in complementary distribution and meet the invariance condition. Then we have /DrD/ in "(two-) eared", "drea(ry)", which is again a violation of buiniqueness, in the usual interpretation. Or, if an exact contrast is wanted, consider the analogous argument with the Low, Back Vowel, and the pair "order"-"drawer". The same kind of problem might well arise in cases of "dissimilation at a distance", which are not rare. In short, we see that the principle of complementary distribution does not even provide a sufficient condition for biuniqueness. Since it provides neither a necessary nor a sufficient condition for biuniqueness, and, apparently, has no motivation except for its connection with biuniqueness, the principle of complementary distribution appears to be devoid of any theoretical significance.

Related questions have been discussed by taxonomic phonemicists, but the general problem has received little attention. Troubetzkoy considers the example of English [r] and [ə], and gives a rule (1935, Rule IV; 1939, Rule IV) that would prevent them from being assigned to the same phoneme in case the sequence [ər] is in contrast with [ə]. This rule, as formulated, is not pertinent to the problem of preserving biuniqueness, and does not cover the examples of the preceding paragraph. It is, furthermore, entirely ad hoc, and thus simply serves to indicate a theoretical inadequacy of taxonomic phonemics.

Among linguists who rely primarily on distributional definitions of the phoneme, apparently only Harris has considered a special case of this problem explicitly. He points out (1951a, 62, note 10) that we might have phonetic representations [ṛay], [kray] for "try", "cry", where t̞-k and ṛ-r are in complementary distribution. But if we were to set up a tentative phonemic system in the manner described above, we could have a phoneme /T/ with allophones [t] before [ṛ] and [k] before [r], and a phoneme /R/ with allophones [ṛ], [r]. But now both "try" and "cry" would be represented /TRay/. To avoid this, Harris suggests that we first group [ṛ] and [r] into /r/, and then redefine distributions in terms of the newly specified contexts, in which [t̞] and [k] now contrast before /r/. This procedure will avoid the difficulty in the particular case of "try", "cry", but not in the cases described above. Furthermore, the same procedure could just as well be used to group [t] and [k] into /T/, thus keeping [ṛ] and [r] phonemically distinct (in further justification, we could point out that this regularizes distributions, since now /t/ occurs neither before /r/ or /l/, instead of, asymmetrically, only before /r/). Hence, as in the case of the procedures discussed above, it fails to distinguish permissible from impermissible applications. Finally, the procedure as stated is inconsistent with Harris' general requirement on the set of linguistic procedures (1951a, 7), namely, that operations must be "carried out for all the elements simultaneously" without any "arbitrary point of departure". In fact, this requirement was what made it possible for Harris to avoid Bloomfield's use of descriptive order (cf. note 35, above). But it is violated by the procedure just discussed.

It is interesting to note that well before the principle of complementary distribution was proposed as the basis of a procedure for phonemic analysis, Jakobson (1931) pointed out the inadequacy of any such principle with a Czech example of exactly the "Scot"-"socked" type given above, and stated as a condition on phonemic analysis that if the phone sequence AB contrasts with BA (see note 17, p. 83), then A and B represent different phonemes (I am indebted to T. Lightner for this reference). Even this condition does not guarantee biuniqueness, because of the adjacency requirement (see above), and is therefore theoretically inadequate. It should be replaced by the simpler condition C: if phone sequences X and Y contrast, then their phonemic representations must differ (Jakobson's condition being a useful special case of this).

To summarize, both taxonomic and systematic phonemic representations must (by definition) meet condition C of the preceding paragraph. But there are no known distributional procedures for defining phonemes that guarantee that this condition will be met, and, in particular, the principle of complementary distribution fails in actual cases. Furthermore, there are no known distributional procedures that permit all analysis meeting condition C and, in particular, the principle of complementary distribution excludes the optimal system meeting C in many real cases. In brief, known procedures of phonemic analyses are unacceptable, and the existence of (still undiscovered) procedures of anything like the sort that have been sought by taxonomic phonemicists is highly dubious.

4.4. CRITERIA FOR SYSTEMATIC PHONEMICS

Systematic phonemics in the sense of Sapir or of § 4.2 does not observe the conditions (32) and is not based on such techniques as complementary distribution or, for that matter, on any analytic procedures of segmentation and classification.[21] Furthermore, construction of the set of ordered rules constituting the phonological component cannot be undertaken in isolation from the study of syntactic processes, just as study of the syntactic compo-

---

[21]   In the case of Sapir, it seems that the choice of examples in his important psychological reality paper (1933) was motivated by his rejection of these (at the time, still unformulated) conditions.

nent cannot be carried to a conclusion without regard for the simplicity and generality of the rules that convert its output into a phonetic representation.

In analyzing a particular language, we must assume given a theory of generative grammar that specifies abstractly the form of grammars and a measure of evaluation for grammars. To fix the level of systematic phonemics for this language, we must attempt to construct the most highly valued grammar compatible with the primary data from this language (cf. § 1). The level of systematic phonemics will consist of the set of representations that appear in derivations provided by this grammar at the point where grammatical morphemes other than junctures have been eliminated. It is certainly conceivable that there exist procedures of some sort that would facilitate the task of selecting this level of representation, but they are not, to my knowledge, available today. It is hardly likely that elementary taxonomic procedures of the kind that have been studied in modern structural linguistics can lead to the discovery of this level of representation. For the present, it seems that the most promising way to give a closer specification of this level of representation and the criteria that determine it is by refining the abstract conditions on the form of generative grammar, the measure of evaluation and the universal features that define the phonetic matrices in terms of which the primary data is represented.

We observed in § 4.2 that if a grammar is to achieve the level of descriptive adequacy, the rules of its phonological component must be ordered; and, in general, a derivation will contain many representations between the systematic phonemic and the systematic phonetic. We suggested that there is no set of intermediate representations that has any systematic significance. Whether or not this is true, we have now, in § 4.3, accumulated evidence showing that if a level meeting the conditions associated with taxonomic phonemics is incorporated in a grammar, then many generalizations will not be expressible and descriptive adequacy cannot be achieved. It is important, then, to see whether there is some way of justifying the assumption that a level of taxonomic phonemics actually constitutes a part of linguistic structure.

4.5. THE MOTIVATION FOR TAXONOMIC PHONEMICS

We are now concerned with the question: why should it be assumed that a grammar must generate representations meeting the conditions (32), as part of the structural descriptions of utterances? What, in other words, is the justification for the theory of taxonomic phonemics, in any of its modern varieties? Many linguists would perhaps take a position of the sort expressed by Twaddell (1935). In opposition to the "mentalistic" approach of Sapir (that is, the approach that is concerned with descriptive and explanatory adequacy), he proposes a method of phonemic analysis for which the following is "the only defense that may be offered": "this procedure ... appears to be characterized by a minimum of the undemonstrable. With one coherent set of assumptions and conventions, which are indispensable to all scientific linguistic study, and one sound laboratory generalization, we may apply strictly mathematical methods and deduce a logically unimpeachable definition of some entity" (74). Thus the phoneme is "a mere terminological convenience" (68). There is no necessity for demonstrating "psychological reality" (i.e., descriptive adequacy), because "this demonstration would be a convenience rather than a necessity for linguistic study: it would represent a summary of the behavior of native speakers, a behavior which is already available for the student of language, though in less concentrated form" (58). The only legitimate activity is "the study of phenomena and their correlations" (57 – this value judgement Twaddell regards as a principle of "scientific methodology"); attempts to provide explanations on the basis of "mentalistic assumptions" are characterized as "fraud". Thus all that may be asked of a linguistic notion or a linguistic description is that it meet the requirement of *consistency* and what we may call *convertibility* (namely, the account must be explicit enough to be convertible into some other, equally arbitrary framework) and, perhaps, in some sense, *simplicity* and *convenience*.

In part, Harris seems to take a similar position in his *Methods* (1951a, chapter 1). He describes his procedures as "merely ways of arranging the original data". The only general condition that they must meet is the biuniqueness condition, which is not justified on any external count, but simply is taken as defining the subject. The procedures must be "based on distribution, and be unambiguous, consistent and subject to check". The criteria for selecting phonemes are stated only "to make explicit in each case what method [of data arrangement] is being followed" (63). Thus only consistency and convertibility (and convenience, for one or another purpose) is required of a linguistic theory or a grammatical description. But Harris also states (372-3) that "the work of analysis leads right up to the statements which enable anyone to synthesize or predict utterances in the language", that is, to a generative grammar. This constitutes a truth claim for the procedures, a claim which surely cannot be maintained if conflicting procedures meeting the conditions of consistency and convertibility are equally valid, and which would appear to be incompatible with Harris' earlier remark that the "overall purpose ... [of the procedures] ... is to obtain a compact one-one representation of the stock of utterances in the corpus" (366). Furthermore, there are no known procedures which lead to this more ambitious, and far more significant goal. These conflicting remarks concerning what Hockett has called "metacriteria" (1955) illustrate a general ambivalence concerning goals that makes evaluation of modern taxonomic linguistics on its own terms rather difficult.

Insofar as consistency and convertibility are taken as the only valid metacriteria, linguistic theory is concerned only with the level of observational adequacy. This theory makes no claim to truth; no evidence conflicts with it, just as none can be offered in its support. The only criticism that is relevant is that taxonomic phonemics, as indicated above, seems more of an inconvenience than a convenience, if embedded within a full grammatical description. This point of view takes a theory to be, essentially, nothing more than a summary of data. In contrast, it has been repeatedly pointed out (most forcefully, by Karl Popper) that the prevailing attitude in the sciences is to regard data as of interest primarily insofar as it has bearing on the choice among alternative theories, and to search for data, however exotic, that will be crucial in this sense. In any event, there is surely no reason why the linguist must necessarily limit himself to "the study of phenomena and their correlations", avoiding any attempt to gain insight into such data by means of an explanatory theory of language, a theory which is, of course, "mentalistic", in that it deals with the character of mental processes rather than with their physical basis.

If one is unwilling to settle for just consistency and convertibility, what further justification can be offered for taxonomic phonemics? I have tried to show above that the internal linguistic evidence does not support taxonomic phonemics. Taxonomic phonemic representations do not contribute to the simplicity or generality of a grammar, but, in fact, have just the opposite effect. Therefore one must search for external evidence. In particular, it is important to ask whether reasonable requirements for a perceptual model ((la) of § 1.3) or a learning or discovery model ((lb) of § 1.3) have any bearing on the validity of taxonomic phonemics. Considerations of this sort may actually have been at the core of some theoretical and methodological studies.

One might try to justify the conditions (32) by arguing that speech perception involves two successive and entirely separate stages: the hearer first uses only local phonetic cues to identify the invariant criterial attributes that determine the successive taxonomic phonemes; and he then goes on to determine the deeper structure of the utterance (in particular, its systematic phonemic representation and its syntactic structure). This clearly seems to be the view of Jakobson (cf. Jakobson, Fant and Halle, 1952) and of Joos (1957, 92)[22] among others. However, there is no real basis for this account, and it is scarcely in accord with what little is known about complex perceptual processes, or, for that matter, about speech perception. Thus it is well-known that intelligibility is preserved under gross

---

[22]   To illustrate his point, Joos cites the example of someone who responded to "he has poise" with "what's a poy?" But this seems rather dubious support for his position, since the hearer in this case was puzzled by the apparent application of the unfamiliar lexical rule: N → poy, and had clearly assigned a full syntactic structure to the utterance. Thus this example does not support the independence of phonemic representation from syntactic structure in perception.

phonetic distortion, which may be completely unnoticed when grammatical constraints are met; and brief exposure to an unfamiliar dialect is often sufficient to overcome unintelligibility or even an impression of strangeness (note that related dialects may differ greatly, sentence by sentence, in phonetic and taxonomic phonemic representations, though perhaps hardly at all on the level of systematic phonemics – cf. in this connection Halle, 1962; also Chomsky, 1959, for an analysis of some of the data presented by Sledd, 1955, 1958, from this point of view). Sapir is the only linguist to have presented careful observations of native perceptual responses relevant to this question, in his classic paper on psychological reality (1933), and his reports are directly counter to the taxonomic account of speech perception. Surely one would expect that in identifying an utterance, the hearer will bring to bear the full grammatical apparatus that determines the space of possibilities from which this utterance is drawn and the nature and interrelations of these objects. That is, one would naturally expect that, as in the case of other perceptual processes, the hearer's knowledge will provide a complex schema within which the actual signal is interpreted. To the extent that this is true, the "atomistic" view of the taxonomic phonologists will be in error. In any event, presently available evidence does not support the taxonomic model given above as an adequate general account of speech perception.[23]

It remains to consider the status of taxonomic phonemics with respect to a model of acquisition of language. There is, in fact, an approach to the question on these grounds.

Suppose that we impose on the acquisition model the condition of *separation of levels*, which we can interpret as requiring that the level of systematic phonetic representation must be "rationalized" and converted to a level of taxonomic phonemic representation without reference to any morphological or syntactic information.[24]

---

[23] For further discussion, see Halle and Stevens (1961), Miller and Chomsky (1963), and references there cited. For discussion in a similar vein on the syntactic level, see Matthews (1961).

[24] One or another form of this is implicit in all substantive discussions of linguistic procedures that I have been able to locate. Some linguists (e.g., Pike and Harris) would allow restricted use of certain higher level information in

Observe that this condition is not to be confused with the conditions of biuniqueness and local determinacy. These (as all of the conditions (32)) pertain to the "perceptual model"; they assert that the phonemic correspondent to a given phonetic sequence must be determinable by operations involving only neighboring sounds, *once the phonemic system is fixed.* But the condition of separation of levels is not a formal condition on a phonemic system and the rules that relate it to sound; it is a methodological condition on information relevant to determining the correct choice of a phonemic system. It thus pertains to an acquisition model such as (lb), rather than to a perceptual model such as (la).

Nevertheless, there is a connection between the condition of separation of levels and the conditions of biuniqueness and local determinacy. If no higher-level information is relevant to determining what is the taxonomic phonemic system, it is natural to require that once the taxonomic phonemic system is fixed, on purely phonetic grounds, no higher-level information should be relevant to determining what is the sequence of taxonomic phonemes corresponding to a given sequence of phones. Consequently, an argument in support of the condition of separation of levels would, indirectly, provide a motivation for imposing the conditions of biuniqueness and local determinacy on the perceptual model as formal conditions on the notion "phoneme".

This is apparently the line of reasoning that has been followed insofar as justification for the conditions of biuniqueness and local determinacy has actually been attempted. Thus, for example, Hockett gives only one argument in support of these conditions in the review cited above (Hockett, 1951), namely, that given these conditions "one knows definitely to what level each fact applies". Otherwise, we have a "hodge-podge arrangement". He is concerned

---

phonology, where this can be obtained by "cyclic" or "spiral" procedures (cf. Pike, 1947, 1952; Harris, 1951a), but many American linguists insist on strict separation. Glossematicians also mention successive and intricately interwoven procedures of analysis and synthesis (Diderichsen, 1958). The kinds of procedures they have in mind also allow for some sort of interdependence of levels, but the reference to procedures is too vague for the extent of permitted interdependence to be determinable, in this case.

here with the context of discovery, not perception, and is offering an argument in support of the condition of separation of levels rather than in support of the biuniqueness and local determinacy conditions directly. Similarly, in his important paper on phonemic overlapping (1941), Bloch offers only one argument (an argument that Joos, in his comment, 1957, considers conclusive) to show why the biuniqueness condition must be maintained, namely, this: "Suppose that we are studying a new and unfamiliar dialect of English, and that we have succeeded in pairing the stressed and the unstressed vowels of such words as *at, them, could, will, so* and the like; if we now hear a phrase like *oút of tówn*, with the unstressed vowel of the second word perceptually the same as those which we have already identified with various stressed alternants, how are we to treat this? We must defer the phonemic analysis until we chance to hear a stressed form of the same word, which may not occur in the dialect we are studying, or which, if it does occur, we may fail to recognize as 'the same word'."

Both Bloch and Hockett are proposing that the condition of biuniqueness must be imposed on the notion "phoneme" because the model for acquisition must meet the condition of separation of levels. But it is important to observe that both of them are presenting an argument that is methodological rather than substantive. They do not suggest that an accurate model of the process of acquisition of language must incorporate the condition of separation of levels – that this is a fact about the design of language and about the intrinsic characteristics of an organism capable of learning a language under the empirically given conditions of time and access. They are considering rather the problems of gathering and organizing data, and thus their indirect argument for the conditions of biuniqueness and local determinacy at most shows that it would be convenient for the linguist if there were a level of representation meeting these conditions, but it does not bear on the question of the existence of this level as a part of linguistic structure.

Let us turn to the question of separation of levels as a substantive issue. As in the case of the conditions (32), two kinds of considerations are relevant: external considerations pertaining, in this case, to language acquisition rather than perception; and purely internal linguistic considerations. As to the former, Hockett has in fact suggested in various places (e.g., 1948) that the successive steps of the analyst should in some way parallel those of the language learner. But clearly the child does not master the phonology before proceeding to the syntax, and there is no possible justification for the principle of separation of levels from considerations of this sort.

It remains then to ask whether this condition can be justified (thus indirectly providing a justification for the biuniqueness and local determinacy conditions) on internal linguistic grounds, that is, by a demonstration that it contributes to the clarity, generality or coherence of a full grammar. But it seems clear that this principle has rather the effect of detracting significantly from these qualities, and, in fact, that adherence to this principle makes it impossible to attain the levels of descriptive or explanatory adequacy. Consequently, the principle seems to be entirely superfluous, in either its stronger or weaker forms (see note 24 on p. 100-101).

The effects of strict application of a principle of separation of levels have often been discussed. The matter of word boundary that Hockett cites in his invented example discussed above on p. 80–81 illustrates the problems that arise when it is adopted. It has long been recognized that a phonemic system is quite unacceptable if no junctures are recognized. Consequently, linguists who adopt the principle of partial or complete separation of levels have attempted to devise analytic procedures that would make it possible to place junctures in appropriate places on the basis of phonetic evidence alone. These procedures make use of phonetic features that appear at utterance boundary to determine the position of junctures medially in utterances. Thus a juncture would be marked in "night rate" because it contains an utterance-final allophone of /t/ followed by an utterance-initial allophone of /r/. Apart from the counter-examples that have already been offered to this principle (and that remain unanswered – cf. e.g., Leopold, 1948; Harris, 1951a, 87; Chomsky, Halle, Lukoff, 1956, § 2) it is clear that it cannot succeed because of examples of the following kind. In many dialects of English, /t/ has the allophone [D] in word final position after a weak stress and before a main stress – thus we have [ɨDédz] ("at Ed's"), [ɨDǽwr] ("at our"), [ðæDǽd] ("that ad"), contrasting with [ɨténd] ("attend"), [ɨtǽk] ("attack", "a tack") and with [ɨdépt] ("adept"), [ɨdǽpt] ("adapt"). But [D] occurs only medially, never finally. Thus any consideration involving utterance boundary will place junctures at exactly the wrong places. Alternatively, if no junctures are placed, [D] must be taken as a third alveolar stop, giving an equally unacceptable phonemic analysis. We must conclude, then, that there is no known method for assigning junctures in terms of phonetic evidence alone. Present methods do not distinguish permissible from impermissible applications, and, consequently, are useless as they stand. It seems unlikely that this difficulty can be remedied, and unless it is, the principle of separation of levels is entirely untenable.

As a second example, consider the much debated subject of English vocalic nuclei. According to ə view that is widely held among American structuralists,[25] these are to be analyzed as short vowels plus one of the glides /y/, /w/ or /h/. On the purely phonetic grounds on which the question must be discussed by those who accept the principle of separation of levels, this is a very neat and well-motivated description. In particular, the post-vocalic /h/, representing a centering glide, can be used to account for such contrasts as "real" /rihl/, "really" /rihliy/ versus "reel" /riyl/, "Greeley" /griyliy/, etc.

If, however, we are concerned with selecting a phonemic system that will be compatible with a full descriptively adequate grammar, this analysis becomes quite unacceptable. Thus observe that on the level of systematic phonemics, the words "real", "really" will be represented /riæl/, /riæl+li/ (because of "reality"), just as "total", "totally" are represented /tōtæl/, /tōtæl+ li/ because of "totality", and "mobile" is represented /mōbil/ because of "mobility". Furthermore, the glide of "real", "really" is the same on the level of systematic phonetics as the reduced vowel of "total", "totally", "mobile" (or, for that matter, "dialect", "betrayal", "refusal",

---

[25] For an account of its background, see Gleason (1961, chapter 19). An important critique is presented in Sledd (1955).

"science", etc.), namely, [i] (there is dialectal variation with respect to height of this vowel that is not relevant here). Hence in all of these cases the systematic phonetic representation can be derived from the systematic phonemic by the very general rule of English phonology that:

(42) Vowel → i when unstressed.[26]

If, however, we wish to provide the taxonomic phonemic representations /rihl/, /rihliy/, /towtil/, /towtiliy/, /mowbil/, /dayilekt/, /biytreyil/, etc., as an intermediate stage of formal description, we must replace the general rule (42) by the three rules:

(43) (i) Vowels → i post-consonantally, when unstressed
     (ii) Vowels → h post-vocalically, when unstressed
     (iii) h → i post-vocalically,

where the first two relate "morphophonemic" and "phonemic" representations, and the third relates "phonemic" and phonetic representations. Thus again we find that what may very well be the optimal taxonomic phonemic system is not incorporable into a descriptively adequate grammar. The failure to achieve descriptive adequacy, in this case, is traceable to the requirement of separation of levels in the underlying theory.

In his review of Halle (1959b), Ferguson (1962) criticizes Halle for his rejection of the biuniqueness and local determinacy conditions (condition (3a) in Halle's presentation), and offers a defense of these conditions. But he presents the issue incorrectly, and as a result neither his critique of Halle's position nor his arguments in support of biuniqueness and local determinacy are to the point. Since Ferguson's is the only recent discussion of this issue from the point of view of taxonomic phonemics, it is important to trace the argument with some care. Ferguson argues for what he calls "the autonomy of phonology", that is, the view that phonology is entirely independent of syntax and morphology, and that the biuniqueness and local determinacy conditions are thus reasonable.

---

[26] This rule is of course incorrect as stated (cf. "relaxation" [rĺlǽkséyšin], "condensation" [kàndĕnséyšin], etc.) if .it is one of a set of unordered rules of a taxonomic grammar. But it is correct if it is embedded into a transformational cycle of the kind discussed above. Cf. references of note 6, p. 14, for details.

Halle's position – and the one that I have advocated here – is the direct contradictory of this, namely, the view that *some* phonetic processes depend on syntactic and morphological structure so that phonology as a whole cannot be studied, without distortion, in total independence of higher level structure. Let us call this the view that phonology is "non-autonomous". A third possible position we may call the assumption of "inseparability of phonology", that is, the view that *all* phonetic processes depend essentially on syntactic and morphological structure. This view has certainly never been advocated by anyone, and it is unnecessary to refute it. But it is the assumption of inseparability of phonology, not the assumption of non-autonomy of phonology, that Ferguson imputes to Halle, and against which he presents a series of arguments (to which we return directly). These arguments against the inseparability of phonology have no bearing on the question of autonomy of phonology. This failure to observe the distinction between inseparability of phonology and non-autonomy of phonology in fact vitiates Ferguson's argument entirely.

Specifically, Ferguson cites in favor of his position the undeniable fact that syntactic and morphological structure are not involved in certain sound changes and in certain aspects of language learning and dialectal variation. This observation is irrelevant to the issue of autonomy or non-autonomy of phonology (though it successfully demolishes the absurd thesis of inseparability of phonology). It also seems apparent that morphology and syntax play an important role in specifying the range and character of certain sound changes (cf. much of Kurylowicz' recent work, or e.g., Twaddell, 1935, p. 79, etc.), of certain aspects of phonological development in language learning, and of certain aspects of phonological dialectal variation. Consequently, to the extent that considerations of the sort that Ferguson adduces are relevant, they show nothing more than the untenability of the thesis of autonomy of phonology. It is true that in plotting isoglosses, "it is often quite clear that subareas of different phonological systems do not coincide well with subareas of grammatical systems and lexical inventories" (Ferguson, 290), just as it is clear that isoglosses drawn for vocalic systems often do not coincide with those drawn for consonantal systems. The argument from this to autonomy is equally apposite in both cases. Similarly, in the case of Ferguson's other examples.[27]

Finally, I should like to comment on Ferguson's assertion that Halle's theory (as also the theory of the present paper) does not provide machinery for describing phonetic data that is accounted for adequately by his autonomous phonology. He cites, e.g., the word *Audrey* with the cluster /dr/ as compared with *bedrock* with /d+r/ and *bedroom* with variation between /dr/ and /d+r/. In this case, a "non-autonomous" generative grammar would give rules stating that in *bedroom* the morpheme boundary sometimes does and sometimes does not become a phonetic juncture (depending on dialect or style, as the facts indicate). It would, on the other hand, make no such statement about *Audrey* (with no boundary) or *bedrock* (where the boundary always becomes phonetic juncture). I do not see what is the problem here, or how an autonomous phonology of the type that Ferguson proposes would handle the situation any differently. Ferguson's example simply shows the absurdity of the claim that *every* morphemic boundary is a phonetic juncture, but surely no one has ever maintained this. What has been maintained is that syntactic and morphological considerations must be taken into account in determining when to handle phonetic facts by placement of junctures and when to handle them by postulation of new phonemes, and Ferguson's remarks have no bearing on this question.

Summarizing, then, it seems that if we are concerned with descriptive and explanatory adequacy, only two levels of representation can be justified in structural descriptions provided by the phonological component, namely, the levels of systematic phone-

[27] Ferguson's claim that a phonological theory that does not observe Halle's condition (3a) (biuniqueness and local determinancy) makes diachronic change incomprehensible is particularly astonishing. Would anyone really be willing to maintain that the phonology of, e.g., Sapir and Bloomfield, cannot accomodate sound changes that have been exhibited and explained by the post-Bloomfieldian linguists who have insisted on these conditions? His assertion that the principles of biuniqueness and local determinacy (note that it is just these that are at issue at this point in his discussion) underlie the achievements of the last century represents a curious interpretation of the history of linguistics.

mics and systematic phonetics. The level of taxonomic phonemics is not incorporable into a descriptively adequate grammar. As noted in § 4.2, this conclusion is close to the position of de Saussure and Sapir, and is close to Bloomfield's practice, though perhaps not his theory.

It is interesting to consider the kinds of criticism that have been offered by taxonomic linguists against de Saussure, Sapir and Bloomfield. Wells (1947) criticizes de Saussure for not making use of the principle of complementary distribution with respect to a particular language in his "phonologie" (but only the analogous principle with respect to all languages). In his long review of Sapir's collected papers (1951b), Harris devotes very little attention to Sapir's theoretical papers on phonology (Sapir, 1925; 1933), and remarks only (293) that they confuse phonology and morphophonemics. Similarly Joos comments (1957, 92) that "when we look back at Bloomfield's work, we are disturbed at this and that, but more than anything else Bloomfield's confusion between phonemes and morphophonemes disturbs us". In the same vein, Twaddell, 1935, in his attempt to counter Sapir's arguments for the psychological reality of the phoneme, dismisses several of Sapir's examples as irrelevant on the curious grounds that they involve morphological, syntactic and lexical information, basing himself, apparently, on the assumption that if certain evidence does not support his own grammar-free concept of the phoneme, then it must also be irrelevant to Sapir's grammar-dependent concept. It is important to observe that these and other critics have not actually demonstrated that the position of de Saussure, Sapir or Bloomfield is in any way confused. The criticism relies on the assumption that systematic phonetics has no significant status (so that de Saussure's phonologie goes only "half way" towards Wells' taxonomic phonemics), and that taxonomic phonemics is a significant intermediate level of linguistic structure (so that Sapir and Bloomfield appear to be confusing morphophonemics and taxonomic phonemics in their systematic phonetics). Hence the criticism amounts only to the comment that de Saussure, Sapir and Bloomfield have not developed the level of taxonomic phonemics, but only the levels of systematic phonetics and systematic phonemics. The criticism, then, is only as well-founded as is the status of taxonomic phonemics.

There is, in fact, a real confusion in Bloomfield, and this has perhaps played a role in the development of taxonomic phonemics in its American version, at least. Bloomfield's assertion that only two kinds of representation are scientifically relevant on the level of sound (cf. above, p. 76 f.) has had a significant impact on later developments. One of Bloomfield's significant levels is physical phonetics. The other, if we follow his descriptive practice, is close to Sapir's systematic phonemics; or, if we follow his "bundle of distinctive features" theory (1933, 79), it is close to post-Bloomfieldian taxonomic phonemics. In any event, he explicitly denies any status to systematic (universal) phonetics. (Similarly, Troubetzkoy, despite his thoroughgoing reliance at every step on a universal phonetics, tends to disparage it in his theoretical remarks.) However, as we noted above, phonology of any sort is unthinkable without assumptions involving phonetic universals, and Bloomfield uses them constantly, as do all phonologists. Hence there are implicit assumptions concerning systematic phonetics in his descriptive and theoretical work. Furthermore, from the rejection of a level of systematic phonetic representation as the "lowest level" of representation to be provided in a grammar, post-Bloomfieldian linguists were forced to the conclusion that the phonemic level must be the lowest level of representation. Consequently, phonemic representation must be much closer to actual sound than in the case of the systematic phonemics of Sapir or of much of Bloomfield's practice. In particular, the conditions (32) become well-motivated, for this lowest level of representation, and the principle of complementary distribution is invoked to eliminate obvious redundancy (supplemented by various ad hoc, and ineffective rules of the kind we have discussed above to take account of cases where the representations meeting (32) are too unintuitive).

In short, we find that there is a gradual return in phonological theory, both American and European, from the systematic phonemics of Sapir and (to a large extent) Bloomfield, to a much "narrower" system not too far removed from that of the phoneticians who were Bloomfield's critics (see note 7). It is in this sense that modern taxonomic phonemic representations are "more accurate" (cf. page 91, above), and it is for this reason that they are far more complex than the earlier systematic phonemic representations. In this way, the fundamental insights of the pioneers of modern phonology have largely been lost.

5

MODELS OF PERCEPTION AND ACQUISITION

A concern with perception and acquisition of language has played a significant role in determining the course of development of linguistic theory, as it should if this theory is ever to have broader scientific significance. But I have tried to show that the basic point of view regarding both perception and acquisition has been much too particularistic and concrete. It has failed totally to come to grips with the "creative" aspect of language use, that is, the ability to form and understand previously unheard sentences. It has, in general, failed to appreciate the degree of internal organization and the intricacy of the system of abstract structures that has been mastered by the learner, and that is brought to bear in understanding, or even identifying utterances. With regard to perceptual models, these limitations reveal themselves in such conditions as linearity, invariance and biuniqueness; with regard to models of acquisition, in such methodological conditions as the principle of separation of levels, the attempt to define grammatical relations in terms of co-occurrence, and, in general, in the emphasis on elementary procedures of segmentation and classification that has dominated modern linguistic theory.[1]

These taxonomic models of acquisition are not far removed from the extremely limited paradigms of learning and concept formation, based exclusively on some notion of matching or similarity or possession of a common property from some fixed set of available properties, that are to be found in recent cognitive psychology. But it does not seem plausible that the kind of generative grammar that seems to be descriptively adequate might be acquired in a reasonably brief time (if at all) by an organism that brings to the learning task only a "quality space" and a "distance measure"

[1] One might cite de Saussure as a source for this preoccupation with inventory and with taxonomic procedures. Cf. (1916, 154).

along these dimensions. Evidence of the kind discussed above suggests that each natural language is a simple and highly systematic realization of a complex and intricate underlying form with highly special and unique properties. To the extent that this observation can be substantiated, it suggests that the structure of the grammar internalized by the learner may be, to a presently quite unexpected degree, a reflection of the general character of his learning capacity rather than the particular course of his experience. It seems not unlikely that the organism brings, as its contribution to acquisition of a particular language, a highly restrictive characterization of a class of generative systems (potential theories) from which the grammar of its language is selected on the basis of the presented linguistic data. There is no a priori reason to expect that these potential theories are of the very simple taxonomic variety with which modern linguistics has been preoccupied, and the linguistic evidence seems to show, in fact, that they are not.

In the case of perception of language, as noted above in § 4.5, the step-by-step analytic models of taxonomic linguistics are not in the least convincing. The process of coming to understand a presented utterance can be quite naturally described, in part, as a process of constructing an internal representation (a "percept") of its full structural description. There is little reason to doubt that the full apparatus of the generative grammar that represents the hearer's linguistic competence is brought to bear immediately in carrying out this task. In particular, much of the perceived phonetic shape of an utterance (e.g., in English, the complex arrangements of reduced and unreduced vowels and stress contours) is a reflection of its syntactic structure. It would not be surprising to find that what the hearer (or the phonetician) perceives is an ideal pattern, not incompatible with the signal that actually reaches his ears, that is projected by the phonological component of his grammar from the syntactic description that he has assigned to this signal (cf. references of note 23, p. 100).

In part, these questions belong to theoretical psychology. But purely linguistic research can play a fundamental role in adding substance to these speculations. A perceptual model that does not incorporate a descriptively adequate generative grammar cannot be taken very seriously. Similarly, the construction of a model of acquisition (whether a model of learning, or a linguistic procedure for discovery of grammars) cannot be seriously undertaken without a clear understanding of the nature of the descriptively adequate grammars that it must provide as output, on the basis of primary linguistic data (cf. § 1.2). It presupposes, in other words, a general linguistic theory that achieves the level of explanatory adequacy. It is clear that we have descriptively adequate grammars, and underlying theories that reach the level of explanatory adequacy, only for a rather narrow range of linguistic phenomena in a small number of languages. It seems to me that present theories of transformational generative grammar provide a basis for extending and deepening our understanding of linguistic structure. In any event, whether or not this hope is ultimately justified, it seems clear that to pursue the goals of § 1 in any serious way, it is necessary to go far beyond the restricted framework of modern taxonomic linguistics and the narrowly-conceived empiricism from which it springs.

BIBLIOGRAPHY

Austin, J., "Ifs and cans", *Proceedings of the British Academy*, Vol. 42. 109–32 (London, British Academy, 1956).

Bar-Hillel, Y., "Logical syntax and semantics", *Language* 30. 230–7 (1954).

Bazell, C. E., *Linguistic form* (Istanbul, Istanbul Press, 1953).

Bever, T. G., "Theoretical implications of Bloomfield's 'Menomini morphophonemics'", *Quarterly Progress Report No. 68*, Research Lab. of Electronics, M.I.T., 197–203 (1963).

——, "The e-o Ablaut in Old English", *Quarterly Progress Report* no. 69, Research Laboratory of Electronics, M.I.T., pp. 203–7 (1943).

——, and Langendoen, T., "The reciprocating cycle of the Indo-European e-o Ablaut", *Quarterly Progress Report* no. 69, Research Laboratory of Electronics, M.I.T., pp. 202–3 (1963).

Bloch, B., "Phonemic overlapping", *American Speech* 16. 278-84 (1941). Reprinted in Joos (1957).

——, "Studies in colloquial Japanese IV: Phonemics" *Language* 26. 86–512 (1950). Reprinted in Joos (1957).

Bloomfield, L., "A set of postulates for the science of language", *Language* 2. 153–64 (1926). Reprinted in Joos (1957).

——, *Language* (New York, Holt, 1933).

——, "Menomini morphophonemics", *Travaux du cercle linguistique de Prague* 8. 105–115 (1939).

Bolinger, D. L., "On defining the morpheme", *Word* 4. 18–23 (1948).

——, "Linguistic science and linguistic engineering", *Word* 16. 374–91 (1960).

——, "Syntactic blends and other matters", *Language* 37. 366–81 (1961).

Bolling, G. M., "Comment on Kent's Review", *Language* 10.48–52 (1934).

Chomsky, N., "Morphophonemics of modern Hebrew" (Univ. of Penna., 1951). Mimeographed unpublished master's thesis, Univ. of Penna., Philadelphia.

——, "The logical structure of linguistic theory", mimeographed (Cambridge, 1955). Unpublished manuscript.

——, *Syntactic Structures* (The Hague, Mouton & Co., 1957a).

——, Review of Jakobson and Halle, *Fundamentals of Language*, in *International Journal of American Linguistics* 23. 234–41 (1957b).

——, "A transformational approach to syntax", *Proceedings of the Third Texas Conference on Problems of Linguistic Analysis in English*, 1958. A. A. Hill, editor (Texas, 1962a), pp. 124–58.

——, "The transformational basis of syntax", submitted to the *Fourth U. Texas Conference* (1959). Unpublished.

——, "On the notion 'rule of grammar'", in Jakobson (ed.), *Structure of language and its mathematical aspects. Proceedings of the 12th Symposium in Applied Mathematics* (Providence, Am. Math. Soc., 1961a), pp. 6–24.

——, "Some methodological remarks on generative grammar", *Word* 17. 219–39 (1961b).

——, "Explanatory models in linguistics", in E. Nagel, P. Suppes, and A. Tarski (eds.), *Logic, Methodology, and Philosophy of Science* (Stanford, Univ. Press, 1962b), 528–550.

——, "Formal properties of grammars", in R. Luce, R. Bush, E. Galanter (eds.), *Handbook of mathematical psychology*, Vol. II, (New York, Wiley & Sons, 1963), pp. 323–418.

Chomsky, N., Halle, M., and Lukoff, F., "On accent and juncture in English", in M. Halle, H. Lunt, H. MacLean (eds.) *For Roman Jakobson* (The Hague, Mouton & Co., 1956), pp. 65–80.

Cordemoy, G., *A philosophicall discourse concerning speech, conformable to the Cartesian principles.* Translated from the French, 1668. The French original (1667) is unavailable to me.

Diderichsen, P., "Morpheme categories in modern Danish", in *Recherches structurales, Travaux du Cercle linguistique de Copenhague*, vol. 5 (1949). non-periodical serial, published by Nordisk Sprog- og Kultur Forlag, Copenhagen, pp. 134–153.

——, "The importance of distribution versus other criteria in linguistic analysis", *Proceedings of the Eighth International Congress of Linguists*, 156–81 (Oslo, 1958).

Firth, J. R., et al., *Studies in linguistic analysis* (Oxford, 1957).

Ferguson, C., Review of Halle, *The sound pattern of Russian*, in *Language* 38. 284–97 (1962).

Foot, P., "Goodness and choice", *Proceedings of the Aristotelian Society, Supplementary volume 35*, 45–80 (1961).

Frei, H., "Désaccords", *Cahiers Ferdinand de Saussure* 18. 35–51 (1961).

Gleason, H. A., *Introduction to descriptive linguistics*, Second edition (New York, H. H. Rinehart, Winston, 1961).

Gleitman, L., Unpublished Master's Thesis, Univ. of Penna. (Philadelphia, 1960).

Godel, R., *Les sources manuscrites du Cours de linguistique générale* (Geneva-Paris, Librairie E. Droz-Librairie Minard, 1957).

Grammaire générale et raisonnée, Lancelot, Arnauld, et al. (Paris, 1660).

Gross, M., On the equivalence of models of language used in the fields of mechanical translation and information retrieval, mimeographed Cambridge, Mass., M.I.T., 1962).

Halle, M., "Questions of linguistics", *Nuovo Cimento* 13. 494–517 (1959a).

——, *The sound pattern of Russian* (The Hague, Mouton & Co., 1959b).

——, "On the role of simplicity in linguistic descriptions", in Jakobson (ed.), *Structure of language and its mathematical aspects, Proceedings of the 12th Symposium in Applied Mathematics* (Providence, 1961a).

——, "Note on cyclically ordered rules in the Russian conjugation", *Quarterly Progress Report No. 63*, Research Lab. of Electronics, M.I.T., 149–55 (1961b).

——, "Phonology in generative grammar", *Word* 18. 54–72 (1962).

——, "On cyclically ordered rules in Russian", *American Contributions to the Fifth International Congress of Slavists* (The Hague, Mouton & Co., 1963), Vol. I, pp. 113-132.

Halle, M. and Chomsky, N., "The morphophonemics of English", *Quarterly Progress Report No. 58* Research Lab. of Electronics, M.I.T., 275–81 (1960).

——, *The sound pattern of English* (New York, Harper and Row, forthcoming).

Halle, M. and Stevens, K., "Speech recognition: a model and a program for research", *IRE Transactions on Information Theory*, IT-8, 155–9 (1962).

Halle, M. and Zeps, V. J., *Latvian Morphology* (forthcoming).

Harris, Z. S., *Methods in structural linguistics* (Chicago, 1951a).

——, Review of Mandelbaum (ed.), *Selected writings of Edward Sapir*, in *Language* 27. 288–332 (1951b).

——, "Discourse analysis", *Language* 28. 18–23 (1952a).

——, "Discourse analysis: a sample text", *Language* 28. 474–94 (1952b).

——, "Distributional structure", *Word* 10. 146–62 (1954).

——, "Co-occurrence and transformation in linguistic structure", *Language* 33. 283–340 (1957).

Haugen, E., "Directions in modern linguistics", *Language* 27.211–22 (1951). Reprinted in Joos (1957).

Hiż, H., "Congrammaticality, batteries of transformations and grammatical categories", in Jakobson (ed.), *Structure of language and its mathematical aspects, Proceedings of the 12th Symposium in Applied Mathematics* (Providence, 1961).

Hockett, C. F., "A note on 'structure'", *International Journal of American linguistics*, 14. 269–71 (1948). Reprinted in Joos (1957).

——, Review of Martinet, *Phonology as functional phonetics*, in *Language* 27. 333–41 (1951).

——, "Two models of grammatical description", *Word* 10. 210–34 (1954). Reprinted in Joos (1957).

——, *A course in modern linguistics* (New York, MacMillan, 1958).

Hoenigswald, H. M., *Language change and linguistic reconstruction* (Chicago, 1960).

Humboldt, W. von, *Über die Verschiedenheit des Menschlichen Sprachbaues* (Berlin, 1836). Facsimile edition, Bonn, 1960.

Jakobson, R., "Phonemic notes on standard Slovak", published in Czech in the Studies presented to Albert Pražák – *Slovenska Miscellanea* (Bratislava, 1931) Now reprinted, in English translation, in R. Jakobson, *Selected Writings*, vol. 1 (The Hague, Mouton and Co., 1962).

Jakobson, R., Fant, G., and Halle, M., *Preliminaries to speech analysis* (Cambridge, Mass., 1952).

Joos, M. (editor), *Readings in Linguistics* (Washington, 1957).

——, "Linguistic prospects in the United States", in Mohrmann, Sommerfelt and Whatmough (eds.), *Trends in European and American linguistics* (Utrecht-Antwerp, Spectrum, 1961).

Juilland, A., *Outline of a General Theory of Structural Relations* (The Hague, Mouton & Co., 1961).

Katz, J. and Fodor, J., "The structure of a semantic theory", *Language*, 39. 170–210 (1963).

Katz, J. and Postal, P., *An integrated theory of linguistic descriptions*. (forthcoming, M.I.T. Press).

Kent, R. G., Review of Bloomfield, *Language*, in *Language* 10 (1934).

Langendoen, T., "The e-o Ablaut in Greek", *Quarterly Progress Report* No. 69, Research Laboratory of Electronics, M.I.T., pp. 207–11 (1963a).

——, *A fragment of Mundari syntax*, M.I.T., 1963b (unpublished).

——, *Modern British linguistics: a study of its theoretical and substantive contributions* (1964). M.I.T. Ph. D. dissertation.

Lees, R. B., *The grammar of English nominalizations* (Bloomington, 1960a).

——, "A multiply ambiguous adjectival construction in English", *Language* 36. 207–21 (1960b).

——, *Phonology of modern standard Turkish* (Bloomington, Indiana 1961).

Leopold, W. F., "German ch", *Language* 24. 179–80 (1948). Reprinted in Joos (1957).

Lightner, T., "Preliminary remarks on the morphophonemic component of Polish", *Quarterly Progress Report* No. 71, Research Laboratory of Electronics, M.I.T., pp. 220-34 (1963).

Long, R., *The sentence and its parts* (Chicago, U. of Chicago Press, 1961).

Malécot, A., "Vowel nasality as a distinctive feature in American English", *Language* 36. 222–9 (1960).

Matthews, G. H., "Analysis by synthesis of sentences of natural languages", *First International Conference on Machine Translation* (Teddington, 1961).

——, *Grammar of Hidatsa*, mimeographed, M.I.T. (1962).

McCawley, J., "Stress and Pitch in the Serbo-Croatian verb", *Quarterly Progress Report* No. 70, Research Laboratory of Electronics, M.I.T., pp. 282–90 (1963).

Mel'chuk, I. A., "Some problems of machine translation abroad", *Doklady na konferentsii po obrabotke informatsii, mashinnomu perevodu i avtomaticheskomu chteniju teksta*, Akademija Nauk, SSSR, no. 6. 1–44 (Moscow, 1961).

Miller, G. A. and Chomsky, N., "Introduction to the formal analysis of natural languages"; and: "Finitary models of language users", both in R. D. Luce, R. Bush, E. Galanter (eds.), *Handbook of mathematical psychology*, Vol. II (New York, John Wiley and Sons, 1963), pp. 269–322 and 419–492.

Miller, G. A., Galanter, E., and Pribram, K. H., *Plans and the structure of behavior* (New York, 1960). Holt.

Newman, S. S., "Behavior patterns in linguistic structure: a case study", in Spier, Hallowell, and Newman (eds.), *Language, culture, and personality*. Sapir Memorial Publication in fund (Menasha, Wisconsin, 1941).

Nida, E. A., *A synopsis of English syntax* (1943). Reprinted, Norman, Oklahoma, (1960).

Nowell-Smith, P., *Ethics* (London, Penguin, 1954).

Palmer, F. R., "Linguistic hierarchy", *Lingua* 7. 225–41 (1958).

Paul, H., *Prinzipien der Sprachgeschichte*, Second edition (1886). Translated into English, Longmans, Green, and Co., London, 1890.

Pike, K. L., "Grammatical prerequisites to phonemic analysis", *Word* 3. 155–72 (1947).

——, "More on grammatical prerequisites", *Word* 8. 106–21 (1952).

Postal, P., "On the limitations of context-free phrase structure description", *Quarterly Progress Report No. 64*, Research Laboratory of Electronics, M.I.T., pp. 231–37, (1961)

——, *Some syntactic rules in Mohawk*, mimeographed (1962). Yale Univ. Ph. D. Dissertation.

——, *Constituent structure: a study of contemporary models of syntactic description* (Bloomington, Indiana University, and The Hague, Mouton & Co, 1964).

Putnam, H. "Some issues in the theory of grammar", in Jakobson (ed.), *Structure of language and its mathematical aspects*, *Proceedings of the 12th Symposium in Applied Mathematics* (Providence, 1961).

Quine, W. V., *Word and object* (Cambridge, Mass., M.I.T. Press, 1960).

Reichling, A., "Principles and methods of syntax: cryptanalytical formalism", *Lingua* 10. 1–17 (1961).

Sapir, E., *Language* (New York, Harcourt, 1921).

——, "Sound patterns in language", *Language* 1. 37–51 (1925). Reprinted in D.G. Mandelbaum (ed.), *Selected Writings of Edward Sapir* (California, 1949).

——, "La réalité psychologique des phonèmes", *Journal de Psychologie Normale et Pathologique* 30. 247–65 (1933). Reprinted in D. G. Mandelbaum (ed.), *Selected Writings of Edward Sapir* (California, 1949).

de Saussure, F., *Cours de linguistique générale* (1916) – page references to the fourth edition (Paris, C. Bally + A. Sechahaye, 1949).

Schachter, P., *A contrastive analysis of English and Pangasinan*, mimeographed (UCLA, 1961).

——, *Rules for a segment of Tagalog grammar*, mimeographed (UCLA, 1962).

Schatz, C. D., "The role of context in the perception of stops", *Language* 30. 47–56 (1954).

Schützenberger, M. P. and Chomsky, N., "The algebraic theory of context-free languages", in P. Braffort and D. Hirschberg (eds.), *Computer programming and formal systems, Studies in Logic* (Amsterdam, North-Holland Publishing Co., 1963), 119–161.

Sledd, J., Review of G. L. Trager and H. L. Smith, *Outline of English structure*, in *Language* 31. 312–35 (1955).

——, "Some questions of English phonology", *Language* 34. 252–8 (1958).

——, *A short introduction to English Grammar* (Chicago, Scott Foresman, 1959).

Smith, C. S., "A class of complex modifiers in English", *Language* 37. 342–65 (1961).

Trubetzkoy, N. S., *Anleitung zu phonologischen Beschreibungen* (Göttingen, Vandenhoeck - Ruprecht, 1935).

——, *Grundzüge der Phonologie* (1939) – page references to the French translation by Cantineau (Paris, 1949).

Twaddell, W. F., *On defining the phoneme* (= *Language Monograph* no. 16) (1935) – page references to reprinting in Joos (1957).

Viertel, J., *The linguistic theories of Humboldt* (in preparation).

Wells, R. S., "De Saussure's system of linguistics", *Word* 3. 1–31 (1947). Reprinted in Joos (1957).

Whitney, W. D., "Steinthal and the psychological theory of language", *North American Review*, 114, 1872. Reprinted in *Oriental and Linguistic Studies* (New York, Scribner, Armstrong & Co., 1874).

Wilkins, J., *An essay towards a real character and a philosophical language* (London, 1668).

Wittgenstein, L., *The Blue and Brown Books* (New York, Harper & Bros, 1958).

Worth, D. S., "Transform analysis of Russian instrumental constructions", *Word* 14. 247–90 (1958).

Ziff, P., *Semantic analysis* (Ithaca, Cornell Univ. Press, 1960a).

——, *On understanding 'understanding utterances'*, mimeographed (Philadelphia, Univ. of Penna., 1960b).

——, *About grammaticalness*, mimeographed (Philadelphia, 1961).